CONTENTS

Foreword   v
Introduction   vii

1. Chapter One   1
2. Chapter Two   30
3. Chapter Three   35
4. Chapter Four   46
5. Chapter Five   67
6. Chapter Six   83
7. Chapter Seven   89

Afterword   117

© Copyright 2019 by Joseph Sorensen

All rights reserved

This document is geared towards providing exact and reliable information with regard to the topic and issue covered. The publication is sold with the idea that the publisher is not required to render accounting, officially permitted, or otherwise, qualified services. If advice is necessary, legal or professional, a practiced individual in the profession should be ordered.

From a Declaration of Principles which was accepted and approved equally by a Committee of the American Bar Association and a Committee of Publishers and Associations.

In no way is it legal to reproduce, duplicate, or transmit any part of this document in either electronic means or in printed format. Recording of this publication is strictly prohibited and any storage of this document is not allowed unless with written permission from the publisher. All rights reserved.

The information provided herein is stated to be truthful and consistent, in that any liability, in terms of inattention or otherwise, by any usage or abuse of any policies, processes, or directions contained within is the solitary and utter responsibility of the recipient reader. Under no circumstances will any legal responsibility or blame be held against the publisher for any reparation, damages, or monetary loss due to the information herein, either directly or indirectly.

Respective authors own all copyrights not held by the publisher.

The information herein is offered for informational purposes solely, and is universal as so. The presentation of the information is without contract or any type of guarantee assurance.

The trademarks that are used are without any consent, and the publication of the trademark is without permission or backing by the trademark owner. All trademarks and brands within this book are for clarifying purposes only and are the owned by the owners themselves, not affiliated with this document.

DISCLAIMER

All erudition contained in this book is given for informational and educational purposes only. The author is not in any way accountable for any results or outcomes that emanate from using this material. Constructive attempts have been made to provide information that is both accurate and effective, but the author is not bound for the accuracy or use/misuse of this information.

FOREWORD

First, I will like to thank you for taking the first step of trusting me and deciding to purchase/read this life-transforming book. Thanks for spending your time and resources on this material.

I can assure you of exact results if you will diligently follow the exact blueprint, I lay bare in the information manual you are currently reading. It has transformed lives, and I strongly believe it will equally transform your own life too.

All the information I presented in this Do It Yourself peace is easy to digest and practice.

INTRODUCTION

Researchers state the normal individual has around 50,000 thoughts per day. Some recommend that 80% or more are negative. For instance, have you at any point had a good thought and thought, "If no one but I could sell it in Walmart or Target, I would make a million dollars?" Then you got occupied and overlooked the thought. At that point a couple of months or after a year you saw your thought on the rack at one of these stores! Another person had the thought, as well, yet they finished. Have you at any point had a sort or adoring word to state to somebody however delayed and after that never said it? Presently you think twice about it. Have you at any point needed something and envisioned about it, however it never occurred?

We had positive considerations, yet they didn't really help. Our inward voice regularly wrecks our endeavors to win throughout everyday life. We get diverted and overlook, or stress over what might occur. Or then again, question executes any great that would happen to it. Would you be able to identify with this? Utilizing a baseball allegory, this is strike one.

If you are attempting to produce the get up and go to push ahead as a result of negative things, the time has come to make positive move. You might haul around sentiments from a mistake, a disappointment, or a negative picture from an earlier time which is hindering you. If that is the situation, remember it, manage it helpfully, and choose to roll out a positive improvement in your reasoning.

Presently, what we are discussing here is the thing that numerous individuals allude to as being stuck, lacking inspiration, feeling stuck, or concentrating on negative feelings. A situation that is normally, pretty much, a transient event. Assuming, in any case, you are managing a worry that goes a lot further than this, don't spare a moment to make sound move and request help from a certified source.

Negative sentiments and pictures that putrefy and are continually returned to can uniquely slow down endeavors to start crisp and push ahead. Both negative and positive mental self-portraits are ground-breaking, and endeavoring to live with both at the same time is a conflict of intellectual prowess that essentially doesn't work. Consider it one counteracting the other.

A cognizant decision to discharge negative considerations and pictures must be made so as to take into consideration new and positive encounters to happen. Doing this enables you to relinquish restricting convictions and to change your point of view. It as a rule expects you to step outside your usual range of familiarity - yet that is the place most achievement truly grabs hold. In this book, I guarantee that you'll get familiar with a self-help guide to manage and overcome social anxiety disorder and improve your social confidence in any situations to live a happy life.

CHAPTER ONE

What Is Mindfulness?

Mindfulness is just a method for being in this world and it very well may be connected to everything that we do. Consider it bringing a totality of experience, comprehension and nearness to our ordinary activities. An immediate meaning of this "nature of being" for what is mindfulness, would be; "a profound present minute consideration, intentionally, without judging or assessing the experience."

Accepting every minute as it comes and valuing it for what it is, without applying judgment or investigation.

A significant part of the science we think today about contemplation has gotten from a scholarly model of preparing in mindfulness that was created at the University of Massachusetts Stress Reduction Clinic (presently known as the Center for Mindfulness).

The subject of what is mindfulness ought to likewise address that it's anything but a religious practice, however has increased critical prominence through Buddhist reflective practices that elevate our capacity to develop mindfulness in our regular day to day existences.

It is fascinating to note too that the meaning of mindfulness as depicted by Harvards Daniel Goleman is fundamentally the same as mindfulness — it is the capacity to see the physical uprising of our feelings in an impartial manner, utilizing this data as an apparatus to react skillfully. For instance the hunch we have when we are desirous, or the strain we experience when we are focused, and so forth.

The incredible thing too that is leaving Yale Universities neuroscience focus the GoBlue undertaking has likewise discovered that from the outset it takes some work to be mindfulness, yet then a point comes in your training where it ends up easy - our minds really move from meandering and always gabbing to a brain that is right now involvement of whatever's going on - loose yet engaged.

The mind is in fact the powerhouse of the entire body. Beside the mind being a reasoning apparatus, it is an interminable wellspring of intensity for wellbeing and life benefits. As an individual, you should be educated on what is mind power and its maximum capacity.

The brain is something other than a group of cells in charge of basic muscle reflexes. It is additionally a memory stockpiling that can procedure up to quadrillion bits of data that even present day PCs can't do. There is an undiscovered asset in each human's mind and for us to increase full profit of its capacity, we should realize how to put it to great use.

The mind has the power control the body's health. Ever wonder why constructive individuals will in general be more beneficial individuals in this planet? It is on the grounds that the positive considerations signal the brain to discharge great hormones to the body. Thinking cheerful considerations is the best anesthesia to wincing torment.

Negative contemplations make terrible impacts to the

body's wellbeing. It triggers the brain to adjust the body's science. If you are as of now debilitated. Negative considerations put on pressure and intensify your physical condition. This is one motivation behind why specialists never enable terrible news to be heard by patients with grave sicknesses. If conceivable, they need wiped out patients to be as agreeable as could reasonably be expected.

The misleading impact is another confirmation of the capacity of mind control. Specialists who comprehend what is mind control in some cases oversee pseudo medicines to patients with stress-related or psychogenic issue. The drug is questionable yet the "prescription" organization gives significant serenity to the patient that the mind shellfishes the body and solaces the body.

Mind power is additionally useful when you are making arrangements for your future. The procedure is called mind molding and it includes practicing the intuitive to accept that the things you need is now accomplished. You condition your mind that you can in reality complete your present College course. Mind molding adds positive support to our objectives with the goal that the errand shows up simple. What you see turns into an inevitable outcome.

Mind power is likewise valuable in vanquishing troubles. The intensity of the mind contributes gravely in facing the issues and putting them down. Individuals who face issues with an unconditioned personality will in general feel sorry for themselves. This procedure makes them ineffective. The most ideal approach to confront trouble is by giving full focus upon the topic and never enables it to administer your life. It is a basic assignment of brain over issue.

If you open yourself to the intensity of the mind, you'll see that you'll welcome the world all the more unmistakably. Beside physical exercise, put on mental activities to extend those mind muscles. Disclose in brainteasers like crosswords, sudoku, and scrabble every so often. Likewise eat protein rich nourishments which are cordial to mind recovery.

What is mind control? It is the utilization of the mind so as to have a superior delight throughout everyday life. It is our desire that you endeavor in making life progressively charming by intuition great considerations.

We as a whole know what contemplation implies, however what explicitly does mindfulness reflection infer? What is mindfulness as per definition? Mindfulness reflection alludes to a psychological express that is portrayed by a quiet mindfulness. The individual encountering mindfulness is absolutely mindful of his own body capacities, emotions, awareness and the substance of his cognizance. Moreover, he knows about such an excess of occurring inside a solitary personality.

Mindfulness is quiet of Buddha instructing, so investigating some essential ideas of Buddhist religion may better get a handle on the definition. Buddha instructs that right mindfulness is a significant part in finding the way to freedom and edification. Mindfulness is additionally the seventh component of the renowned Noble Eightfold Path. A content known as the Satipatthana Sutta is a content that manages mindfulness and related ways of thinking. One of the significant lessons of Buddha was that this sort of mindfulness ought to be joined with profound reflection to the point of retention.

In spite of the fact that this strategy started in eastern grounds, it has as of late turned out to be well known in western progress and in different brain research disciplines. There are two principle parts in mindfulness. The first of these is known as self-guideline of consideration. The objective here is to keep up consideration just on the quick experience, as in the now minute. This takes into consideration an upgraded capacity to perceive mental occasions occurring in the present. The subsequent segment includes taking a specific view towards present minute encounters; a view, a direction, of interest, receptiveness with one's self, and all out acknowledgment.

The primary segment of mindfulness includes having a cognizant familiarity with one's present contemplations, emotions and condition. This outcomes in an individual creating what is designated "metacognitive abilities" so as to more readily control focus. The subsequent part includes an individual tolerating his very own mind stream and keeping up open and inquisitive perspectives towards all convictions and things; moreover, it includes thinking in elective classes.

Mindfulness is a training that anybody can rapidly learn and quickly use to profit one's psychological, physical, and passionate wellbeing. On the off chance that you have considered doing reflection or beginning a mindfulness preparing program however didn't know what it implied then this article will be incredible at clarifying the essentials of mindfulness before beginning practice.

What is Mindfulness?

In the West, the field of brain research has built up a restorative work on beginning during the 1970s called mindfulness. It has establishes in the Buddhist contemplation routine with regard to mindfulness. Customarily, in Theravada Buddhism, individuals could be shown two types of contemplation which mirror the cutting edge routine with regard to mindfulness.

The first is a quieting of the mind practice which for the most part includes watching one's breath go in and out. Is it true that you are breathing through your nose or your mouth? Through your correct nostril, your left nostril, or both? Full breaths or shallow breaths? This type of reflection helps settle the mind and bring the individual over into the present minute without such a large number of unpleasant, irregular considerations and development. This type of reflection is predominantly to carry a quiet harmony to the brain and monitoring one's contemplations and body.

The second is a type of contemplation is called knowledge or vipassana reflection. Knowledge contemplation includes effectively watching one's self including one's musings and body sensations without judging or assessing them as fortunate or unfortunate. What's more, thusly, one starts to disentangle the main drivers of these marvels.

In the present mindfulness practice in Western brain science, these components are safeguarded in staying alert right now and having a non-judgmental frame of mind towards whatever is going on. Fundamentally, it is figuring out how to hold one's consideration and focus without judgment along these lines being progressively mindful of the present and being increasingly open and tolerating to whatever occurs.

What the Benefits of Mindfulness Practice?

Mindfulness treatments have indicated incredible guarantee for various therapeutic and mental conditions. These incorporate issues, for example, constant agony, tension/sorrow, and stress. Intellectual treatment could be considered to exemplify numerous mindfulness standards as far as monitoring one's contemplations. Basically, mindfulness is a routine with regard to changing one's negative mental propensities so it tends to be helpful for any assortment of conditions, for example, sedate maltreatment or extreme sadness.

Is Mindfulness a Form of Buddhism? Would anyone be able to Do It?

All things considered, mindfulness as clarified prior is certainly inside the Buddhist conventional practices. Numerous educators, for example, Shunryu Suzuki and Thich Nhat Hanh have acquainted Buddhist reflections with the West which straightforwardly propelled the present types of mindfulness in brain science and treatment. Be that as it may, one could apparently discover various variations of mindfulness practice in every single otherworldly custom. Since the real practice itself is just an open attention to the present minute, there are no convictions or authoritative opinions that one needs first. But maybe a receptiveness to analysis and readiness to trust it may be conceivable to bring emotional changes through mindfulness practice.

Mindfulness is a psychological practice that anybody can do and would support everybody. It doesn't need to be associated with any religion and can bring prompt positive outcomes at the present time. In any case, it is regularly exceptionally supportive to initially learn mindfulness with an educator to ensure you are doing it accurately.

We're altogether overpowered with data consistently. Some is new data that we're relied upon to learn and recall; some is data with respect to an issue for which we're required to discover an answer.

The greater part of us don't have opportunity to spend obsessing about this data long enough to remember it with customary strategies, or to completely comprehend and fuse the majority of the features of an issue that we need to explain.

Things being what they are, how would we understand that ceaseless torrential slide of material?

Simply: with a little method called "Mind Mapping."

They have turned out to be well known on the grounds that they help us to sort out the information that overpowers us every day, and transform that information into significant learning.

Sharp Mind Mappers can be found all over:

You'll discover understudies Mind Mapping their notes, businessmen Mind Mapping ventures and gatherings, and Web engineers making advancement activities and Web destinations utilizing them.

In case you're mindful of them, yet don't yet utilize them,

odds are that this is on the grounds that you believe they're unpredictable to learn, and you're too occupied to even consider bothering contributing the time.

Whatever framework you're utilizing now to complete your work works (in spite of the fact that it could be progressively compelling) — what will Mind Mapping accomplish for you to reimburse the time you put resources into learning?

Mind Mapping can help you in each aspect of your life and work. It can make you increasingly productive, by helping you to accomplish work all the more rapidly; it can push you to issue explain, and beat difficulties; it can assist you with finding arrangements, on the grounds that the appropriate response is consistently in the issue; and it can assist you with learning new data, and improve your memory.

Basically, a Mind Map is an outline, which encourages you to think.

It shows your thoughts in a visual structure, for the most part around a focal word, expression or picture.

Albeit utilized for quite a long time, Mind Maps were promoted by creators like Tony Buzan around 30 years back, and are currently generally utilized in business and in instruction. When you utilize a Map, it's simpler to recall data, but on the other hand it's simpler to make associations between unique thoughts and grow new ideas.

They work since they include the two sides of your brain in the manner of thinking.

The left half of your brain is the sensible, levelheaded side, and the correct side is the side that works with inventiveness and imaginativeness.

While the left half of your brain is attempting to take mindfulness of an issue with sanity and rationale, the pictures and imagery of the Mind Map help to include the correct side of your brain in the critical thinking process, for predominant outcomes.

They help you to maintain a strategic distance from straight reasoning; records are excessively precise, and are in this way unreasonable, since issues are scattered and multi-faceted.

At the point when individuals make records, they frequently delay continually to ensure that they're not missing anything, and that everything is in the correct grouping; this prompts investigation loss of motion, where you are so occupied with examining what you have composed that you don't complete anything.

They additionally help you to see the 10,000 foot view, and see how all pieces of an issue are interrelated.

One of my preferred statements is the well known line spoken by Napoleon Hill in Think and Grow Rich: "What the mind can consider and accept, the brain can accomplish."

Sounds great isn't that right?

At the point when our brains acknowledge that something is valid, a conviction, at that point our outlooks moving any occasions to make that our existence.

Whatever convictions, considerations, and thoughts that your brain gets comfortable with, or is molded to, must turn into a piece of you and that is who you moved toward becoming.

Be that as it may, how would we get our brains to consider and accept, and at last accomplish, the things we need?

The mind resembles having our very own little PC - it just hurls out outcomes dependent on the directions we give it.

When we need various outcomes, we should give our brains new directions to pursue.

Some call it self-proposal, others call it auto-recommendation, others call it subliminal informing, yet I like the term reframing.

Reframing is the point at which you consistently bring new thoughts and musings into your mind until they become a predominant conviction.

The measure of time it takes to reframe new convictions into your mind will rely upon how reliably you present new contemplations versus the measure of time you spend considering your present convictions.

Envision some messy water (your flow convictions). If you start to include clean water (new considerations) to the cup, in the long run you will wind up with some perfect water (new convictions).

It additionally relies upon the measure of convictions you have in your mind that should be reframed. Supplanting some filthy water takes less time that supplanting something the size of a bath, or a pool.

Convictions are actually simply contemplations — thoughts that we believe are valid. Actually convictions are not certainties, they are just contemplations. Sure they may look like certainties on the grounds that our external world has been organized to coordinate our convictions.

We can think and accept anything we desire.

The more we think another idea, the more it turns into a conviction. When these new convictions have turned into a piece of our inner mind, at that point our reality must change to coordinate our new convictions.

"WHAT THE BRAIN CAN IMAGINE AND ACCEPT, THE MIND CAN accomplish."

Instructions to know and work with your mind utilizing mindfulness based methodologies

Today a significant number of us are battling with pressure. Feeling a feeling of feebleness, feeling overpowered by all we need to do, an absence of certainty, no time, monetary stresses. No opportunity to play with our kids, no time for our friends and family, no time for ourselves. Crushed presently, pressed in our resilience, feeling a feeling of detachment and division from our central cores.

I know this personally in light of the fact that I've encountered these things myself filling in as an instructor of English in the UK. Anyway I had been rehearsing mindfulness and reflection for a long time. I have given a great deal of idea to how to apply mindfulness to the worries of life and I have prepared in mindfulness ways to deal with pressure, torment and disease as an authorize Breathworks mentor.

So I am in a situation to discuss what mindfulness is and how we do it.

Mindfulness is a multi year aptitude, a craft of life. As a method for working with our brains, we are seeing it being recovered by present day prescription as a method for managing pressure, agony and despondency without falling back on medications treatment.

In any case, mindfulness can makes our lives more extravagant, increasingly innovative, progressively intentional and hence more joyful paying little respect to what our identity is, the thing that religion we are, regardless of whether we are religious by any means, what our circumstance is, the thing that our beginning stage is.

So what is Mindfulness? This is an exceptionally enormous subject and it's what my Living Well with Stress and Living Well with Pain and Illness are altogether founded on. Mindfulness can be an extremely grand subject but on the other hand it's very basic, it is basically, memory. Simply re-gathering the Mind which has strayed in to a universe of idea, a mind that has gone personality less — re-gathering it back together in the now so we can make the following stride with inventiveness and respectability and satisfy our higher reason in this life, our spirit reason.

We once in a while do things mindfully where we have our mindfulness in that spot and we're accomplishing something in the now, present to ourselves, we're there seeing it. At that point a ton of the time, we're off, we're doing things thoughtlessly, we've lost ourselves in something we are doing or in some line of idea, very some story we've made.

So the craft of Mindfulness is to returned to the present. Just to give a case of the distinction as connected to how we can take a gander at how we may do a basic assignment like wash the dishes. We as a whole need to do it.

This is the means by which we could do it. We could be in the present getting a charge out of the vibe of the water, acknowledging we have hot, clean water, appreciating truly getting into working admirably, getting things spotless and sudsy, appreciating the rainbows in the air pockets, the whiteness of the cleanser suds. Cleanser suds, the white frothy foaminess that cleaning up fluid makes. We could be getting a charge out of suddenness of cleanser suds, making an intensive showing, perhaps with cleaning up fluid which is environmentally inviting, appreciating the plants on the window ledge. We can be doing this in a present manner and the activity moves toward becoming something tasteful and in light of the fact that we're available we can know about our bodies and our vitality and life power and we can appreciate this as well. What's more, we can know about our souls, mindful of the individuals who are our closest and dearest and with whom we are sharing our lives. We can know about our affection for them.

That is one method for doing it. Be that as it may, how would we do it more often than not? We would prefer as a rule not to do it, we think that it's dreary and undesirable and we do it perhaps reluctantly and we turn off and go down some idea course and lose ourselves in idea universes. These idea universes are frequently not universes of light and life tragically. They are regularly our musings fuelled by tension, stress and even neurosis, or include some craving or aching by which we can escape from the truth of what our lives are and who is in them. This is a Big subject.

Be that as it may, the primary concern is to recall, abruptly the light returns on and we are back. Here, in the present. With the goal that we can be in a greater consciousness of the now and not lost in the stressing mazes of idea. So we can be in contact with our motivation, with our friends and family in an extremely open manner.

So we can either be here, present and open to our experience, with a mind like the blue sky with a wide scene, Or we can be in limited focus, lost in stress and our mindfulness has shut right in, here and there so firmly individuals take there possess lives in light of the fact that in their idea, their downturn, their pressure they have lost the master plan.

It's somewhat similar to a retractable focal point, mindfulness.

This is something we chip away at in my Living Well with Stress and Living Well with Pain and Illness courses.

So how would we do it? I'm going to give you the mystery, the system that it's taken me such a long time to get to myself. This is something basic, anybody can do it, on the off chance that you have a body, you can do it.

It is essentially to come into the body. Come into your experience of your body and out of your head. It's something you may not in any case perceive if your experience isn't in your body, and you're up in your mind in your idea universes constantly. Yet, it feels totally unique if your experience is found not in your mind.

I went through more than 40 years in my mind and it was anything but an especially charming spot to be. We're especially given to this in the west I think since we have a mind-heart split and we think mind is found just in the brain. In any case, astounding and superb as the mind may be, we are conscious, we have insight, intelligence in each cell of our body. The human heart is delicate. We know things all the more profoundly regularly from coming into our souls, our guts, these spots have neurons in them, similar to the brain does.

We are designed for profound knowing all through our body, we should have been the point at which we were trackers and were following creatures and all aspects of our body needed to tune in and be delicate so we could tune in out for and track wild creatures without being heard by them. Our lives relied upon this and however we carry on with the life of settled agrarian network now, we are still from a developmental perspective tracker gatherers. The timeframe since the revelation of agribusiness is just 0.4 percent of our transformative history, only a squint in the developmental eye. So these faculties are totally recoverable to us.

What's more, this is uplifting news, we should be epitomized for some reasons. One significant reason is that our wellbeing relies upon it. It's when we don't tune in to our bodies, it's when what we know is subsumed by advanced pressure that we get sick. Disease is regularly a way our body has of causing us to end up mindful of it.

Being in the body is significant so we can be in contact with our vitality and our life power. It feels great when you feel this. You may feel it, not that everybody doesn't but rather individuals are getting worried and debilitated in light of the fact that they are not tuning in to their body. Being in contact with your body I would state is the most significant thing for your wellbeing, bliss and your survival. That is my most significant message — to tune in to the body.

A great deal of my courses are to do only this, since it requires some serious energy and practice and that is a ton of what we're doing on these courses.

That is all I have opportunity to state about this significant subject for the time being but to leave you with a grin, about the cleaning up. I was doing the cleaning up and conversing with my companion, and I turned towards her adage something very genuine no uncertainty and I had a whiskers of cleanser suds all round my face. It was so absurd, we chuckled and snickered. So she says when she'll generally consider me wearing a facial hair of cleanser suds, so consider me too when you're doing the cleaning up with my cleanser suds whiskers. We would all be able to be unaware, we would all be able to return to that snapshot of mindfulness and decision with the goal that we can make the inventive next stride. That imaginative subsequent stage may be to giggle and have a great time in whatever we're doing.

What Is Mind control — it sounds great; the sort of stuff that everyone needs and it is something that is being discussed to an ever increasing extent. Yet, what is mind control and what does it truly mean?

When I read or hear the words: mind control, an image shapes in my brain of me utilizing my considerations to shaft some undetectable power out at some objective and cause it to do what I need. It's a typical understanding and I'm speculating it's not very not at all like what you're envisioning either. It's an influential thought that catches and feeds our creative mind, and it is portrayed and fortified on and on in motion pictures, books, canvases, and comics....

It is an idea that we as a whole promptly comprehend, on the grounds that it is something we naturally know is genuine and once in a while we experience verification of it. We consider something that we need, we forget about it, and a couple of days after the fact it appears in our life, as a rule in an unforeseen manner. We consider somebody we haven't been in contact for quite a while, the telephone rings, and it is their truism "hi" on the opposite end. When it happens its incredible, a rush, however we've no thought how it occurred or how to get it going once more, and when we attempt it doesn't work.

Having these encounters isn't encountering genuine personality control. It is just having a look at an internal potential that we as a whole have, however which is in the greater part of us immature. When you have genuine personality control you turned out to be progressively ready to utilize it in an anticipated and controlled way, and see as well, that there can be a hole between hitting your objective and encountering the planned outcome.

Having this sort of mind power is conceivable, and some have it, or are along the way to having it. However, the fact of the matter is the vast majority will never have it since they are not willing to take the necessary steps to create it. Building up one's mind power requires some investment, requiring tolerance, and determination. It is a genuine duty yet the prizes are exceptional.

That is a stacked inquiry. The exceptionally fundamental answer that will profit you incredibly in knowing is that the more profound degrees of awareness that are in charge of the more programmed parts of reasoning are extremely amazing in impacting our lives. This implies we don't for the most part deliberately even see what happens when our more profound degrees of our brains are grinding away. This is significant on the grounds that we can really get to, increment, program, improve and change our subliminal brain so it will naturally offer us the response to the inquiry "what is mind control".

This advantages we all incredibly. I know for a fact that once you start to deliberately build your subliminal capacities you will consequently find what is mind control; you will end up more joyful, things will turn out to be all the more clear, issues become simpler so they don't raise such ruckus, arrangements become more clear, errands complete snappier and everything in life just appears to show signs of improvement.

So how would I increment subliminal solidarity to know the response to the inquiry "what is mind control"?

That is a generally excellent inquiry; anyway we need a little history first. There are numerous individuals who have made sense of that you can really speak with and impact the lower levels of awareness. This has turned out to be extremely impeding to our mind. The individuals who are voracious and need to keep control are really utilizing control to lead the majority into a condition of need. This means a large portion of us are instructed from a youthful age to look to other purported "specialists" to take mindfulness of the majority of our issues. This prompts such huge numbers of issues up to and including extreme discouragement.

There is trust.

So as to turn around this procedure and start expanding our command over our mind; we have to start to program ourselves all the time. We will start to see the appropriate response that will uncover what is mind control. This is impossible until we know in our bones that we have this capacity. We have to persuade ourselves on all degrees of our awareness that we have the quality. This is a troublesome accomplishment to perform without the best possible assistance. It is difficult to turn around long stretches of nonstop programming. Positive reasoning systems alone will work after a significant lot of time; anyway for a speedier and more secure technique a considerable lot of us have gone to brainwave entrainment.

With brainwave entrainment; deductively verified binaural beats are utilized to even out the various sides of the equator of the mind. These thoughtful beats really bring the person into Zen-like expresses that expansion the minds movement and correspondence causing increased conditions of quickened learning capacities. With brainwave entrainment an individual turns out to be incredibly powerless to recommendation and programming. After an individual is brought into a Zen-like thoughtful state it turns out to be fairly simple to program and exploit the person's subliminal. We would then be able to start to comprehend the response to the inquiry "what is mind control". With the individual lifted into a higher condition of awareness we would now be able to start the positive attestations to survive and crash the long periods of negative programming.

Following a little while of re-programming you will start to naturally contend with the negative musings that emerge. At whatever point an idea emerges, for example, "that is excessively hard, I will always be unable to do that"; you naturally begin to address yourself. You start to begin searching for the answer for issues. You start to wonder why it is that you can't do the things that appear to be so difficult. You start to really begin working out potential cures. This may appear to be confounding from the outset; anyway it is actually very straightforward. We have been customized from a youthful age to uncertainty are capacities. The main contrast between somebody who succeeds and a disappointment is question. An individual who succeeds realizes that they will succeed and thusly places the majority of their vitality into doing precisely that.

This is the genuine quality of our intuitive and will uncover what is mind control!

After you start having confidence in yourself and investing a little energy consistently on progress; you start to feel good, think all the more obviously, have less pressure, manage circumstances in a progressively gainful manner, discover answers for issues with astounding pace and have an overall better life. You do need to invest a tad bit of energy consistently on the grounds that there are hindrances toward each path. Lamentably the individuals who are in power are terrified of losing it. They will make every effort to keep you subjugated. This is anything but difficult to see once you start to deal with your subliminal uncover "what is mind control".

When you take part in the brainwave entrainment strategies you will start to assume responsibility for your life and predetermination. It is a quite extraordinary inclination to realize that you are the ace of your predetermination. I was discouraged to the point of suicide before I started to assume responsibility for my life. This used to be a hard thing for me to concede, anyway I am so sure (not yielded) and cheerful since I can be straightforward with anyone who I interact with. Everything begins with making a move towards making a superior life.

You may have heard the expression "Mindfulness" and have an unpleasant thought of what it's about yet in this article, you'll get an unmistakable comprehension of what it is and why it's imperative to you.

Mindfulness is that hole where you, the mindfulness, know about what's going on inside your brain. You become clear and alarm to what you think, say and do. Regularly individuals reflect as a method for being more clear without every one of the diversions the flood through the faculties. Be that as it may, getting to be mindful of your breath and concentrating reporting in real time streaming all through the lungs can likewise do it.

This may not seem like any major ordeal, however it's a fantastic jump of what some other animal can do. People are the main species on this planet that can do this. This is on the grounds that each different species doesn't relate to the mind to make a sense of self, they basically acknowledge things as they are and are unified with it.

For instance, a feline doesn't stay there and figure, what does that human consider me, would it be advisable for me to make my jacket shinier so he'll pat me and give me sustenance? No, they basically acknowledge this minute and do what they do through impulse and being in arrangement with the present minute.

Along these lines creatures have a favorable position over people, yet what we have is the following period of development, where we have a stunning ability to make due as well as flourish prefer no different species.

The issue is however, our journey to endure and flourish has turned out to be out of offset with our basic nature of unity with all. This irregularity makes us experience torment, which at last drives us to scan for as well as to discover what the Truth is for us. It's life's method for reestablishing harmony and when you think about that we are not separate to life, it's our method for reestablishing harmony inside ourselves.

So would you be able to perceive any reason why this is significant at this point?

Basically, the fantasy of living everyday through totally mind based action (more often than not in expectation or in dread that tomorrow will be not the same as today) causes torment, NOW. The best approach to start to discover your way through the torment is to carry attention to your breath and from that point, seeing what you think, say and do. The mindfulness makes a hole among you and what is seen and through that a decision can be made for what is genuine, you the mindfulness or what your brain is letting you know through an observation!

I regularly observe it in the money related markets, where the market will move toward a path (allows state to down) and what everybody sees through the mind is dread and conceivable misfortune. At the point when this gets to an extraordinary, individuals are so entrapped with the mind that they don't perceive some other decision however to sell at a misfortune so as to stop the agony. The expert then again, sees how dread and voracity hold individuals, so they kick back and pause and afterward profit by deal costs. They have the decision to do this since they see the hole among the real world and what is seen. It's enjoyable to watch!

ow do we increment the level of mind power utilized so we can more readily control our lives and improve our circumstance and eventually make the way of life and achievement that we long for?

There are a few manners by which you can deal with your brain and tackle the power and have progressively positive encounters.

This requires the utilization of the correct aptitudes and apparatuses that can enable you to accomplish the degree of mind control that can realize a total extraordinary change.

THERE ARE SURE PUTS ON THE PLANET, FOR EXAMPLE, THE Himalayas, India and Tibet, which are viewed as home to more prominent positive vitality levels and can enable you to accomplish an a lot higher perspective and a higher personality power level.

Be that as it may, you can accomplish an a lot higher personality power level without venturing out to these nations. You can do it directly from your own room or even while sitting in a seat.

That is its excellence. You have total access to this power whenever you need. Everything necessary is a touch of training, order and some assurance on your part.

For instance, you can...
Contemplate
Imagine
What's more, you can rehearse self-entrancing strategies for better fixation and center, to hone your brain and develop your mind control. Your musings, which structure some portion of your brain, have mind boggling power. This

power can transform yourself in a moment once you figure out how to take advantage of it.

This is the reason a portion of the contemplations that simply appear to fly into your brain, can really materialize. That is the intensity of your brain.

In this manner, when you put a portion of your psychological vitality into having some positive and incredible musings once a day, similar to the day by day insistences procedure they will become more grounded and in the long run influence your practices, your activities, and your frame of mind, and keeping in mind that raising your desires, achieving fabulous outcomes.

With training, when you become gifted at taking advantage of, and utilizing your subliminal personality, you will at that point start to discover and see openings and perfect circumstances emerging out of the blue, you will see people around you appear to be unwittingly or purposely, helping you, managing you, and offering you the open doors you look for around then.

Our subliminal personality makes the results dependent on our contemplations and convictions. We can in some cases name these results as an "occurrence", a happenstance that brings into your life positive occasions and incredible chances.

Mindfulness means focusing on the present minute with a non-judgmental, non-receptive and tolerating frame of mind.

The focal standards of Mindfulness are known as composure and fleetingness.

Serenity implies an unbiased reaction to something we experience. It is a condition of mindfulness where we neither feel a revulsion for unsavory experience nor longing for wonderful ones. Different methods for portraying Equanimity are parity, tranquility, and self-control.

Fleetingness implies the changing idea of all things

including our own musings and emotions. By encountering the changing idea of inward encounters, we can disengage ourselves from unbending perspectives that can once in a while lead to pressure and despondency.

Do you perceive how mindfulness can be useful for dietary problem's treatment? It encourages us to build up the condition of equalization or serenity where we neither feel a repugnance for undesirable experience nor needing for charming ones.

When you go on a gorge, just before you start you generally have these staggering sentiments of longings for sustenance. Before starving yourself you have sentiments of revulsion or sicken with yourself and your body — so you quit eating.

With mindfulness you will have the option to see your dietary issue as a remote voice (or an individual) who is sitting inside you, instructing you. When you practice mindfulness you will have the option to isolate yourself from this outside voice and be free.

Mindfulness is a subset of contemplation rehearses. To be mindful most importantly you should figure out how to think. Mindfulness and contemplation are comparative however not actually the equivalent. Like we have just clarified that mindfulness is the familiarity with the present minute. Be that as it may, Meditation is simply the purposeful guideline of consideration. During reflection you manage and control your consideration. What's more, this is an advancement of mindfulness.

In mindfulness you learn not to pass judgment and not to respond. Seeing what goes by nonjudgmentally, from minute to minute, with no reactivity at all towards any piece of the experience, regardless of whether the idea or the sensation. By diminishing our overactivity in the judgmental piece of the brain and the receptive piece of the mind, our sensory system figures out how to change its example. It turns out to be less judgmental, less receptive, increasingly objective, giving us more chances to oversee life whatever the issue is.

This strategy isn't constrained to dietary issues, nerves, fears or sadness. Individuals of various religions practice this technique in various ways for a large number of years. This is surely not constrained to mental or passionate issues.

Everybody will profit by diminishing reactivity, diminishing one-sided decisions, giving new parameters to the sensory system, and more knowledge and centered consideration. Basically, the motivation behind rehearsing mindfulness preparing is to build up a level of acknowledgment towards one's understanding, and obviously an equivalent level of mindfulness. At the point when things become satisfactory within, it appears that individuals discover things increasingly adequate outwardly also. The world improves as a spot.

Mindfulness is something contrary to thoughtlessness, and by and large means being mindful and accommodating, rather than being indiscreet and impolite. Mindfulness is tied in with monitoring what's going on right now.

The most ideal human services starts with self consideration which enables you to apply some authority over your very own prosperity. Rehearsing mindfulness is a groundbreaking methods for playing a functioning job in your very own self consideration and improving your general condition of wellbeing.

Mindfulness has extended from its profound roots to turn into a system that numerous doctors are supporting to manage pressure related conditions that as often as possible lead to torment and diseases running from generally mellow to extremely serious. Analysts have discovered that mindfulness offers a method for looking at impulsive reasoning and presenting available resources that counter over the top idea. It has turned out to be obvious that numerous individuals are not so much controlling their considerations to such an extent as being controlled by their musings.

Along these lines, mindfulness is tied in with preparing to live in the present time and place. To be available, instead of to be continually practicing for what may occur later on, or repeating what has occurred before. Stressing is another word for it. When you consider it, the present minute is the main spot that life can be appropriately delighted in light of the fact that it is all that truly exists. Mindfulness has been formed into a framework that gives preparing about embracing the here and now. It is a method for being loose and mindful as opposed to being stressed and unstable.

Tragically numerous individuals are uninformed that they are absent and attempting to live previously or later on, which just exist in their very own preconditioned personalities. We have all observed individuals strolling about looking just as they have the world on their shoulders instead of getting a charge out of the daylight or the ocean breezes or the trees or the blossoms or whatever. They are distracted with the past or the future yet on the off chance that you haven't saw them it might be on the grounds that you are one of them. These circumstances are the place mindfulness makes its mark to puncture the cloak of thoughtlessness and let the light radiate through.

Luckily mindfulness courses are promptly accessible and it isn't too hard to address urgent reasoning examples. Numerous books have been composed regarding the matter and a Google search of mindfulness will create a large group of assets that are prepared to help with fighting the anxieties brought about by thoughtlessness. For the individuals who require a progressively close to home course there are an expanding number of mindfulness mentors running courses that have helped many worried people.

Since mindfulness is demonstrating to be such a superb methods for mitigating pressure and the torment and illnesses related with it, it is winding up progressively well known. It is conveyed by expert individuals in restorative focuses in the United States and somewhere else and some enormous organizations have acknowledged how helpful it tends to be for their administrators and others that they are presenting in house courses. When such a significant number of pressure related conditions are treated with physician endorsed medications, and others are self sedating with substance misuse, or going to liquor, it is extraordinary to have the option to report that less obtrusive and exceptionally fruitful different medicines are accessible.

A basic clarification of Mind-Body Psychology is the means by which the mind influences the body. There is substantially more to this rapidly creating field. A superior elucidating name would be Mind-Body-Spirit Psychology, with brain consolidating both the reasoning and passionate parts of the person. The interrelationship between the brain and the body have consistently been stowing away before us. Presently specialists are concentrating on this association and finding the power every individual has inside them to influence their body just by controlling musings, feelings and winding up profoundly mindful.

Specialists used to, and I'm certain many still do, say something is "all in your mind" when they can't locate a physical purpose behind an agony. The term utilized is "psychosomatic." What is occurring in your brain is influencing your body.

Presently it is generally acknowledged that pressure can have a negative and dangerous impact upon the physical piece of yourself. For example, hypertension is as often as possible pressure related. I recall my father, a pediatrician, saying that his circulatory strain fell 10 when he resigned. One regular pressure related physical issue is muscle torment which is the immediate consequences of straining the muscles when pushed.

Dread has a particular impact upon the body. Circulatory strain rises, assimilation stops, sex drive vanishes and the insusceptible framework debilitates. This has all been exhibited by logical research. When you feel dread the body trusts it's in peril and should plan something quick for spare itself. The outcome is closing down every single superfluous arrangement of the body (absorption, sex and resistant) to give it more vitality to focus on enduring the now.

THE ISSUE IS THAT THE PRESENT CURRENT RISK ISN'T A SABER tooth tiger that will before long be gone. It is longer enduring feelings of trepidation. This keeps the battle or flight component constantly activated.

This is the reason dealing with the feelings and contemplations to quiet the body is so significant. Dread can prompt flee musings. For example, you hear gossip there will be layoffs. You become apprehensive you'll be one to lose your employment. You quickly structure pictures of being out in the city with no spot to go and nothing to eat. Your physical self, accepting your feelings of dread for what's to come are a present threat, reacts with the pressure responses referenced previously.

When you figure out how to remain in the present with brief visits to the future to make arrangements, you keep your brain from over-responding and moving you into stress. It's urgent to shield yourself from thinking about each conceivable negative thing that could occur on the off chance that you lose your employment. It's certain to build up a long haul plan for a budgetary fiasco by consistently placing cash in a stormy day finance.

On the off chance that you have perused or generally been presented to the theme of health, you have likewise likely progressed toward becoming in any event passingly acquainted with the act of mindfulness. It has, as of late, relocated from being to some degree a periphery enthusiasm for some alt-wellbeing experts to being a decently standard methodology. However, what is it, and how can it work?

There is anything but a solitary definition for mindfulness. My top pick, and the one set forth by a pioneer of the utilization of mindfulness in restorative settings, is the accompanying:

"Mindfulness means focusing with a certain goal in mind; intentionally, right now, and nonjudgmentally."

This definition unquestionably has the goodness of quickness. Albeit brief, it gets at the center segments of mindfulness. It is a straightforward practice, shockingly so. What's more, before developing the definition, it is additionally essential to give some unique circumstance.

Mindfulness is compelling. It is powerful as a way to diminish pressure, oversee ceaseless agony, or manage mental difficulties. As the training has moved into the standard, it has gotten progressively basic consideration from researchers and analysts. As a helpful practice, it is by all accounts holding up quite well. The University of Wisconsin Department of Family Medicine has a summary of an inspecting of the exploration accessible on the remedial applications for mindfulness here. The University of Massachusetts community for Mindfulness, the home of the previously mentioned Jon Kabat-Zinn, has a comparative summary of companion looked into research they have distributed on the advantages of mindfulness. At last, here is a concise report from the UCLA Mindful Awareness Research Center that offers a summary of the ebb and flow condition of mindfulness explore in different zones of human working.

This isn't intended to be an extensive outline. Positively, there is still work to be done in deciding how and when mindfulness is most useful, and in characterizing restrictions for the training. However, you can see that in any event three noteworthy national research organizations, UW, UMASS and UCLA, are giving mindfulness significant consideration.

Anyway, back to the more commonsense inquiries, what is it, and how is it helpful? It isn't any kind of shrewd understanding to see that we live in a quick paced, occupied, associated world. Between family time, work, family support, different interests, leisure activities and different commitments, once in a while the business on our plate outpaces our capacity to keep up. Add to that the consistent association of remote gadgets, when we are accessible to others about day in and day out, and you have a circumstance where we absolutely never sit still for long. This ethic of consistent association and diversion has so woven itself into the texture of day by day life, that it is difficult to envision existence without it.

Mindfulness includes backing ourselves off enough to really encounter what is happening in our brains and our bodies at the present time, or, if you like, continuously. It resembles developing a little piece of ourselves that, rather than being driven around by the ear by our interests, impulses and gadgets, makes a stride back and really focuses on what is happening, and whether we are occupied with our lives such that we need to be. You could consider it like this: mindfulness is the remedy to auto-pilot.

CHAPTER TWO

The Purpose Of Mindfulness

We all experience change constantly. Consistently. Change is the main consistent nowadays. It occurs and it happens quick. What are you doing pretty much the majority of the adjustment in your life? It is safe to say that you are opposing it? Giving it a chance to wash by you? Grasping it? Giving it a chance to take you where it will? I envision that a large portion of us do these things dependent on the change that is occurring at the time. Be that as it may, what might it resemble on the off chance that we were more accountable for our reactions to change? What might it resemble on the off chance that we were increasingly out before it?

We can be on the off chance that we choose to lead a mindfulness and purposeful life. By driving a mindfulness and purposeful life I mean having an unmistakable mission, vision and set of qualities that guide our life and utilizing that to control by. When we utilize our own main goal, vision and qualities to manage us they act like a rudder giving us strength and helping us make course revisions as life gets extreme. They help us set our course when the going is smooth so as we see change seemingly within easy reach we have an approach to settle on choices about that change and can make sense of how to utilize it to further our potential benefit as opposed to consider it to be an immense hindrance.

Mindfulness and aim go past simply having an individual mission, vision and qualities. It is reflected by they way we approach our day by day living. It is reflected in the objectives we set for ourselves and by they way we approach achieving those objectives. Aim comes in with respect to how we address objective fulfillment. How are we going to approach accomplishing our objectives? How are we going to treat other individuals along the way? What is our goal with each activity that we choose to take. What is our goal with our responses to things? Deliberate individuals have a genuine reason set out about how they are going to appear on the planet and how they will associate with the individuals in it.

At last mindfulness becomes possibly the most important factor. A mindfulness individual is constantly mindful of himself and how he is collaborating with other individuals. He is completely mindful of how his activities sway others and of how they respond to him. He screens that and connects with his expectations to increase a beneficial outcome and result.

So you see goal and mindfulness have an inseparable tie to change - being responsible for the results of progress is a ground-breaking thing. Making sense of this isn't in every case simple. This may be an extraordinary time for you to get a mentor to help.

What is Mindfulness Meditation?

Mindfulness contemplation is a psychological preparing practice that includes concentrating your brain on your encounters (like your own feelings, musings, and sensations) right now.

Mindfulness reflection can include breathing practice, mental symbolism, familiarity with body and brain, and muscle and body unwinding.

One of the first institutionalized projects for mindfulness contemplation is the Mindfulness-Based Stress Reduction (MBSR) program, created by Jon Kabat-Zinn, PhD (who was an understudy of Buddhist priest and researcher Thich Nhat Hanh). MBSR centers around mindfulness and consideration regarding the present. Other streamlined, common mindfulness reflection mediations have been progressively joined into medicinal settings to treat pressure, torment, a sleeping disorder, and other wellbeing conditions.

Learning mindfulness intercession is direct, in any case, an instructor or program can help you as you start (especially in case you're doing it for wellbeing purposes). A few people do it for 10 minutes, yet even a couple of minutes consistently can have any kind of effect. Here is a fundamental method for you to begin:

1. Locate a peaceful and agreeable spot. Sit in a seat or on the floor with your head, neck, and back straight however not firm.

2. Attempt to set aside all memories and the future and remain in the present.

3. Become mindful of your breath, concentrating on the impression of air moving all through your body as you relax. Feel your stomach rise and fall, and the air enter your noses and leave your mouth. Focus on the manner in which every breath changes and is extraordinary.

4. Watch each idea travel every which way, regardless of whether it be a stress, dread, tension or expectation. At the point when considerations come up in your brain, don't disregard or smother them however essentially note them, keep quiet and utilize your breathing as a grapple.

5. If you end up escaping in your musings, see where your mind headed out to, without judging, and basically come back to your relaxing. Keep in mind not to be no picnic for yourself if this occurs.

6. As the opportunity arrives to a nearby, sit for a moment or two, getting to be mindful of where you are. Get up slowly.

Different Ways to Incorporate Mindfulness Into Your Life:

There's no law that says you should sit on a pad in a tranquil space to rehearse mindfulness, says Kate Hanley, creator of A Year of Daily Calm. Mindfulness intercession is one procedure, yet every day life gives a lot of chances to practice.3

Here are Kate Hanley's tips on developing mindfulness in your day by day schedule:

Doing the dishes. Have you at any point seen how nobody is attempting to stand out enough to be noticed while you're doing the dishes? The blend of alone time and physical action causes tidying to up after supper an incredible time to attempt a little mindfulness.

Brushing your teeth. You can't go a day without brushing your teeth, making this every day task the ideal chance to rehearse mindfulness. Feel your feet on the floor, the brush in your grasp, your arm going here and there. Einstein said he did his best reasoning while he was shaving- - I'd contend that what he was truly doing in those minutes was rehearsing mindfulness!

Driving. It's anything but difficult to daydream while you're driving, considering what to have for supper or what you neglected to do at work that day. Utilize your forces of mindfulness to keep your consideration moored to within your vehicle.

Mood killer the radio (or go it to something mitigating, similar to old style), envision your spine developing tall, locate the midpoint between loosening up your hands and holding the wheel too firmly, and take your consideration back to where you and your vehicle are in space at whatever point you see your mind meandering.

Working out. Truly, sitting in front of the TV while running on the treadmill will cause your exercise to go all the more rapidly, however it won't do a lot to calm your brain. Make your wellness attempts an activity in mindfulness by killing all screens and concentrating on your breathing and where your feet are in space as you move.

Sleep time. Watch your fights over sleep time with the children vanish when you quit attempting to hurry through it and basically attempt to appreciate the experience. Get down to a similar level as your children, look in their eyes, listen more than you talk, and appreciate any cuddles you get. When you unwind, they will as well.

CHAPTER THREE

Efficient Ways To Implement Stress Management

Deal with Your Stress
Stress is known to be one of the most widely recognized reasons for ailment in our general public today, thusly you have to figure out how to deal with your stress. Stress is in charge of the breakdowns seeing someone at work, school and at home which at that point lead to health issues Learn how to limit, lighten or wipe out stress in your life. It is presently perceived in the business field that stress-related issues are one of the most widely recognized reasons for non-appearance in the work place.

SIGNIFICANT CORPORATIONS ARE CURRENTLY PERCEIVING THE need to deal with your stress and are executing stress decreases programs in the work place. Stop and check out what's going on in your life right now.

Deal with your Stress in regular day to day existence.

Observe the things that happen each day that directly affect your stress levels. Before we can manage the issues that stress makes in our lives, we have to perceive and comprehend what is happening, see what exists and after that build up an arrangement and treat the fundamental causes.

STRESS IS ALL OVER. REGARDLESS OF WHETHER YOU ARE A worker, a chief, jobless or an understudy, you experience a wide range of stress in your life. Whatever your calling or status throughout everyday life, you can't flee from stress. In any case, there are approaches to adapt to the stress. Stress management incorporates approaches to manage the day by day weight of life. With the correct disposition, you can carry on with a without stress life in the midst of your stressful condition.

DISTINGUISH THE SOURCES OF STRESS IN YOUR LIFE

The underlying advance in stress management is to know the wellsprings of stress in your life. Albeit a few sources are inescapable, you can make approaches to decrease them. In any case, if the wellspring of your stress is avoidable, attempt to discover approaches to keep away from the stressful circumstance with the source.

DUE DATES

The standard wellspring of stress from work and school works is complying with the time constraint. Be it a report or a task, it is sufficient to give you stresses. A viable stress management in gathering due dates is to take a shot at the undertaking as right on time as could be expected under the circumstances. When you get the undertaking, attempt to take a shot at it the soonest conceivable time to avert a propensity for continually beating the due date. Along these lines you can even have additional opportunity to survey your work, coming about to unrivaled reports and papers.

Pointless Responsibilities

Another regular wellspring of stress is the point at which you acknowledge obligations that are beyond what you can tolerate. Successful stress management shows individuals how to state no. By just disapproving of obligations, you lessen the measure of stress in your life. Nobody can say what amount is sufficient. Anytime you believe you can't offer time to an additional duty, saying no is the best alternative.

Learn Healthier Ways to Manage Stress

A few people manage stress by smoking, crying, gorging or undereating and drinking excessively. Despite the fact that this may happen now and again, consistent utilization of these methodologies will cause you more stress than any other time in recent memory. When you anticipate stress or experience it, attempt different stress management systems. Take a walk, have an exercise custom, write in your diary or play with your pet. These are healthier approaches to stress management. Utilizing the systems, you calm your stress without hurting your body.

Managing stress proficiently is the way to endure an incredible requests. By learning stress management, you can all the more likely adapt to it. You possibly have two choices with regards to this, it is it is possible that you stop the stress or the stress will murder you. It is your decision and you should make the correct one.

. . .

Stress Management - A Healthy Lifestyle Equals a Healthy Workplace

Stress can have hindering consequences for an individual's body just as their life. Stress brings down the insusceptible framework, in this way debilitating the body's guards. The individual turns out to be increasingly vulnerable to numerous conceivably hazardous afflictions.

The impacts of stress shift from individual to individual. One individual may build up a moderately sensible sickness, for example, a gastrointestinal condition, while others may encounter all the more conceivably hazardous illness, for example, hypertension or coronary illness. Contingent upon exactly how much stress an individual is encountering, a few conditions may emerge all the while. This is the reason legitimate stress management ought to be learned and rehearsed consistently.

There are numerous approaches to actualize stress management into one's life. One route is by recalling not to take work home. Regardless of whether you work out of your home, it is critical to isolate office time from individual time. Permitting an adequate measure of time every day to appropriately loosen up and unwind is an extraordinary stress management strategy. Investing quality energy with family, perusing a decent book or cleaning up are extraordinary approaches to decrease stress.

Exercise is another brilliant stress management strategy. There doesn't need to essentially be any sort of formal exercise program, just fusing strolling, biking or notwithstanding cultivating into your life will do the trick. Also, the more pleasant the exercise, the more viable it will be. Many pick yoga as a strategy for stress management. This is a particularly brilliant decision since yoga isn't just physical however it likewise includes the mind and soul all in all. Whenever rehearsed all the time, this can be exceptionally recuperating for the body.

SOME OF THE TIME THE MOST VALUABLE STRATEGY FOR STRESS management is just keeping stressful occasions from occurring in any case. For instance, a work environment could hold an obligatory reoccurring meeting to enable all representatives to voice their sentiments about how things are going and to give criticism. This avoids stress by empowering everybody to talk about issues that may have been irritating them and potentially resolve the issues.

ONE MORE APPROACH TO COUNTERACT OR DIMINISH THE measure of stress in the work environment is by guaranteeing that there are sufficient representatives to finish assignments in a sensible timeframe. At the point when laborers are surged and need to comply with almost outlandish time constraints all the time, this puts the representatives under a lot of weight, which could bring about expanded sicknesses. It is significant that businesses cling to this, in such a case that a lot of their workers are out on wiped out leave, there will be next to no profitability.

ON THE OFF CHANCE THAT BUSINESSES HAVE POSITIVELY NO decision yet to push their representatives to comply with a significant time constraint, at that point an appropriate method for giving stress management during this period could be offering paid downtime and rewards to compensate the diligent work. On the off chance that this kind of stress management can't be used, at that point maybe an elective method for loosening up after such a stressful time can be utilized.

LEGITIMATE AND NORMAL STRESS MANAGEMENT SHOULD BE fused into the lives of everybody, regardless of whether they are a housewife with three kids or a CEO of a noteworthy organization. Stress management isn't significant for a healthy way of life, yet additionally to improve proficiency at the work environment.

The Easy Stress Management Techniques

These are amazing methods that are anything but difficult to learn and they don't take a great deal of time or exertion. As soon as you notice you don't have opportunity to tune in to a guided unwinding CD, or take an interest in an exercise program or ponder for 30 minutes every day, at that point these procedures will give you a brisk method to start to battle the impacts of stress. No reasons, everybody possesses energy for this stuff so how about we get the chance to work!

PROCEDURES I - JUST BREATHE!

I have individuals approaching me always for straightforward stress management methods to bring some relief. Let's be honest, we are pushing ahead at a pace today that overrides anything in mankind's history. What's more, if I'm not mistaken, we are not doing so well. Simply read the most recent insights with respect to our health in this nation and the pattern is stunning. We are accomplishing more with less assets and attempting to fit it all in at a completely rankling pace...something must give! All the most recent data and investigation demonstrates to us that the conventional everyday stress in our lives is in charge of 66% of every one of specialists' visits! People, that is everything from the basic cold to coronary illness and malignant growth, and if stress isn't the essential driver of the issue, it is absolutely a contributing component.

I KNOW FROM INDIVIDUAL ENCOUNTERS THE IMPACTS THAT stress can have on the body and our emotional wellness. By a wide margin the most significant stress management strategy I generally show individuals initially includes basic relaxing! I recognize what you are thinking...you are as of now breathing throughout the day. Genuine, however the majority of you are doing everything incorrectly!

I WILL WATCH MY ASSOCIATES WHILE THEY ARE COMPOSING, seriously centered on some venture. Their breathing is so shallow it's astounding they can even support their life! Not exclusively is their breathing shallow, yet it is additionally for the most part finished with the upper chest. This isn't an effective method to inhale and it loots the collection of valuable oxygen. Presently I don't think about you, however I'm truly excited oxygen is without still and since I'm not paying for it I'm going to take in as much as I can. With regards to breathing you can spend lavishly and be insatiable!

LEGITIMATE BREATHING STARTS IN THE STOMACH. THE stomach goes about as a cries in the body and as it grows it maneuvers air into the lungs. Filling the lungs appropriately will furnish you with astounding outcomes in decreasing stress. All that oxygenated tissue will help each procedure of the body including your capacity to center, digest sustenance, and loosen up muscles, just to give some examples. And for all intents and purposes, each part of your physical and psychological well-being can be improved with legitimate relaxing.

How about we investigate how we can take an appropriate breath. Put one hand on your chest and your other hand on your stomach. Presently take in a full and complete breath, filling your lungs with however much air as could be expected. When you have got done with breathing in at that point breathe out, keeping your hands set up. Take another breath and this time give close consideration to how your hands move. What you're going for is to have the hand on the stomach move outward from the body first as the lungs load up with air. As more air fills the lungs then the advantage should move outward from the body as your chest extends. When you breathe out the hand on the chest should move in before the hand on the stomach and you ought to breathe out completely and totally.

I would prescribe you take 40 full breaths consistently. Incidentally, don't do this at the same time except if you appreciate feeling faint, I don't need you hyperventilating and going out! I like to pick something to remind myself to relax. Ordinarily, I watch the clock and that can make me begin to feel stress as solid pressure coming into the body. Thus, every time I wind up checking the time, I interruption to take a full diaphragmatic breath. I additionally utilize this method when the telephone rings, so before I answer I have taken a full breath and felt a flood of unwinding wash over me. It truly causes me plan for whatever I might confront. This additionally functions admirably for those occasions I feel that outrage going ahead because of the day by day open doors for self-awareness and development my multi year old girls' dramatization brings into my life.

You can't locate a simpler system that can accomplish such a great deal for controlling stress. Attempt this for yourself for the following week. Make the promise to change this one part of your life and you will start to see the intensity of straightforward stress management strategies. To a limited extent two of this article we will investigate the intensity of setting a positive expectation

Systems II - Shake it, Shake it!

One of the most widely recognized territories of the body where we will in general hold stress is the strong framework. Stress can make the muscles actually contract and fix, regularly prompting fits and genuine torment. Most of individuals feel this pressure in the upper back and neck and they can encounter everything from a mellow consuming sensation to weakening agony. Frequently, this is the antecedent to pressure cerebral pains and it can truly upset our lives.

The greatest issue with strong strain issues is to get the issue before it shows itself as solid torment or cerebral pains. The most concerning issue with this is it very well may be hard to anticipate when this will happen in light of the fact that the torment appears to simply abruptly show up. Be that as it may, it is conceivable to figure out how to feel the strain sneaking in on the off chance that we simply give more consideration to our bodies. In this way, we should investigate how to actually shake that pressure out!

. . .

Alright, stand up, give yourself a lot of room and attempt this examination. Start to tenderly shake your correct hand at the wrist. Attempt to seclude only the wrist as you let the pressure start to shake out. Your fingers ought to be free and floppy. Keep in mind, this is a delicate shaking; you are making an effort not to win a challenge here. Do this for around 15 seconds or somewhere in the vicinity and afterward incorporate the lower arm up to the elbow as you keep on shaking. Once more, attempt to let the strain simply wash away as the arm is truly free and floppy. Proceed with like this for an additional 15 seconds. At that point incorporate the entire right arm, as far as possible up to the shoulder. Everything in the arm is free and floppy now as you delicately shake away any staying strain. Make an effort not to oppose at all and see exactly how free you can make the muscles in your arm. Do this for an additional 15 seconds and afterward stop.

Presently simply let your arm hang down. Look in a mirror and you if you have done this accurately your correct arm will be recognizable longer than the left! You may likewise see a beating or shivering sensation in your fingertips and your hand may even feel warm and flushed. This is on the grounds that you have freed yourself of the choking strong strain that was available in the arm and blood and vitality are presently streaming all the more effectively enabling the arm to feel progressively loose. You have truly shaken the pressure out of the arm and in doing this have stepped toward loosening up your body and dealing with your stress.

You will need to rehash this on the opposite side of the body so you have balance. You can do this in the legs also, beginning with the foot and lower leg and stirring your way up the leg until it is all shaking. When doing the leg shaking it is a smart thought to relentless yourself on a divider or seat so you don't free your equalization. You many need to consider a private spot to shake out the strain except if you need some weird looks and conceivable undesirable consideration! Obviously, if you do this in a bank on a Friday evening, you are ensured to move ideal to the front of the line!

Alright, since the arms and legs are free, you can move to some delicate shoulder shrugs, neck turns and some other developments and delicate extending that you like to do to help release the storage compartment muscles. On the off chance that you are composing or stuck at a work station throughout the day I prescribe doing these exercises about once an hour to keep the pressure under control and you can do them as frequently as you like consistently. Simply make sure to keep everything delicate, free and loose and clearly stop if you feel any torment or unsteadiness.

Presently you are along the way to lessening solid pressure. Allow it to shake, shake and roll.

CHAPTER FOUR

A Guide to Stress Management for Workaholics

Obsessive workers are more inclined to being influenced by stress than the others since they spend longer hours working in stressful conditions. The expanded burden, which is regularly the situation with obsessive workers, can be distressing and can agitate your effectiveness, and thus, your efficiency. This is an endless loop since stress will prompt less profitability and yield, which thus may bring about discontent and eagerness causing more stress and the hover goes on. This is the reason for obsessive workers, successful stress management is basic to their exhibition.

STRESS MANAGEMENT DOESN'T REQUIRE A UNIQUE SPOT OR time to be actualized; it tends to be drilled anyplace, whenever - at your home, at work, even in the vehicle, or when you are cooking or out for a walk. Try to sneak some loosening up exercises in ordinary interims into your timetable. They don't should be long and tedious; just a couple of minutes of de-stressing can do some amazing things.

HERE ARE A FEW HINTS:

TIP # 1: DETERMINE THE WELLSPRING OF YOUR STRESS

The undeniable initial move towards disposing of the stress is to discover what is causing it. It very well may be your partners, your chief, and trouble of the task close by or some other factor. Take out a couple of minute and show them out with the goal that you can deal with them later and in the end take mindfulness of the issue.

TIP # 2: RELAXING YOUR MIND

Unwinding is the indispensable advance for fruitful management. Having a casual mind will bring about an unmistakable and progressively engaged mind. This makes taking mindfulness of the issues simpler since you can think with a straight mind and see things with a reasonable head. Breathing exercises, light meditation or even a stroll in the natural air for a couple of minutes can assist you with loosening up. You need to attempt to quit pondering the issue. Enjoy a reprieve and afterward start over again.

YOGA AND MEDITATION HAVE BEEN DEMONSTRATED TO BE incredible apparatuses for unwinding. The best thing about this is you need not spend a ton on it. Be aware that anytime you have no earlier information you can essentially take in it from self-help books or the web in your extra time.

. . .

Tip # 3: Pamper yourself

Utilize your extra time admirably. Spoiling yourself in a spa is a brilliant and sure approach to unwind. Regardless of whether you don't get a full-body broad spa treatment, a straightforward back rub, the sauna, fragrance based treatment or even a basic hot shower with loosening up salts can do ponders. The result is that you feel loose, refreshed and new. Prepared to confront your issues.

Stress Management - A Critical Factor of Successful Corporate Change

Everybody is set in circumstances that require changing their way of life, thought examples and employment condition. For some these progressions happen consistently. For some they happen once in a while. Be that as it may, one thing is without a doubt, change ALWAYS causes stress at different levels. Taken mindfulness of accurately it very well may be made a joy and a wellspring of individual and gathering pride. The present flood in expert change management in organizations requires some cautious thought with regards with the impacts of that stress on the people and their association.

Our reality has made tremendous changes in the course of recent years. The resultant stresses are causing genuine mental and physical health issues that thusly convert into tremendous financial expense at individual, business and government levels. By taking mindfulness of the PERCEPTION of the change appropriately, a lot of unnecessary anxiety and genuine results can be stayed away from. The view of progress and its normal results must be comprehended by the person at an oblivious level all together for the stresses to be diminished to a base. This is an altogether different procedure to exhibiting the requirement for change just at a cognizant level and expecting the person's memory and qualities framework to acknowledge it.

THE OBSERVATION THAT INDIVIDUAL CHANGE IS DISTINCTIVE TO authoritative change is wrong. Both have a similar impact whenever taken mindfulness of wrongly, at the end of the day an association acts in the very same manner as an individual experiencing change. The main genuine contrast is that in close to home change the stress emerges from struggle between poorly educated parts regarding the mind, while stress in hierarchical change is gotten from clashes between parts of the association (different minds). Where the two sections struggle at an individual level and parts strife at a hierarchical level happen, intense outcomes will be shown.

IN THE TWO CIRCUMSTANCES THE VALUES SYSTEM OF THE individual parts should be perceived and sometimes adjusted before stress levels because of progress can be decreased. Utilizing exceptionally propelled strategies of methodology assessment, we would now be able to distinguish potential clashes before a change system is instituted, diminishing the potential for disharmony and individual stress. The monetary advantages of this become obvious when you consider the genuine expense of ailment and staff turnover of an association.

TREATMENT OF BOTH INDIVIDUAL CHANGE AND AUTHORITATIVE change needs to consider the people in a change procedure as people. This includes understanding various elements including:

- Values frameworks
- Ability - specialized and learning
- Previous history of progress
- Reaction to verifiable change
- Perception of proposed change
- Perception of work associates
- Perception of the people place in the association
- Ability to coordinate innovation change
- Assessing the innate culture of an association indicates the verifiable advancement of the association, yet additionally to the management style and social collaboration set up.
- The second most significant segment of dealing with change incorporates an appraisal of:
- What additional business dangers are presented through the change?
- The genuine requirement for change to happen
- The speed with which change needs to happen
- Based on the previous history and desires for staff, will the change be viewed as positive or negative from their perspective?
- Does the change include innovation overhauls that will require higher ranges of abilities?
- Does the staff expected to incorporate the innovation change have the ability to do as such?
- Will viable preparing staff be accessible to move abilities required?
- Will the organization or association give the assets to guarantee the instruction procedure required by people PRIOR to change being actualized?

GIVEN A COMPREHENSION OF THESE COMPONENTS, A GREAT change supervisor will have the option to build up a profoundly successful custom program to execute any sort of progress. This applies whether the change is actualized by a specialist on an individual level, or an administrator on an authoritative level.

IN AN ASSOCIATION EACH LEVEL, FROM SENIOR MANAGEMENT through to mindfulness staff must be assessed for their capacity to actualize and set changes required. Frequently, management perceive the way that "something" is turning out badly, however have no clue how to fix the issue. Experience demonstrates that this level is so engaged in the everyday running of the business from a specialized and corporate administration viewpoint, they disregard the way that the authoritative living being is comprised of individuals.

IT IS A MIX-UP TO ACCEPT THAT PEOPLE CAN ONLY "JOB WITH the punches" and acknowledge any change foisted upon them. It is additionally an error to make a decent attempt offer procedures to pass on the requirement for change. These systems don't work and never have. Those individuals may have broadly differing qualities frameworks and the resultant clash makes abnormal amounts of anxiety, outrage and gloom in associations, prompting low efficiency, significant staff turnover and high disease levels. The sicknesses are indistinguishable to the issues introduced to me every day as an advisor and stress management specialist.

FOR A FACT, IT IS REGULARLY HIGH STRESS LEVELS IN management expedited by apparent execution desires that must be managed first. Without clear course and arranging and correspondence, significant changes can be viewed as "the absolute last thing that could be tolerated" in center management. This regularly undermines the achievement of presented change in an association.

A DECENT CHANGE MANAGER IS COMPLETELY MINDFUL OF these issues at an individual level and sets up compelling methodologies to deal with the potential aftermath from enormous scale change before the change is executed. He/she at that point must screen the whole procedure until the individual and association return in a steady situation. By doing this enormous potential misfortunes can be kept away from and the ideal outcome from the change will be seen sooner in the reality.

WHEN THE HAZARD EVALUATION HAS BEEN FINISHED AND AN altered authoritative advancement plan has been settled upon, the arrangement is actualized in the accompanying request:

1. SENIOR MANAGEMENT IS INSTRUCTED IN WHAT'S IN STORE and how to react to difficulties and protection from the proposed change.

2. SECOND LEVEL MANAGEMENT IS PREPARED IN THE necessities for presentation of new frameworks or advancements so they are seen by staff to be compatible with the organizations results and are a piece of the usage.

3. INSTRUCTIONAL COURSES FOR EACH GATHERING OF STAFF individuals is executed in a manner that doesn't disturb

everyday business to a harming degree. This preparation considers the insight assembled about these gatherings and their probability to oppose the change, acknowledge a move in organization strategy or effectiveness or become some portion of a general cultivating of recharged pride and security in a consistent professional workplace. This preparation is upheld by customary correspondences to all staff on the advancement and particularly in the adjustment in client or other partner's view of the revived organization.

4. FRAMEWORKS AND ADVANCES ARE EXECUTED IN AN organized procedure and level of acknowledgment and combination is checked by the change management and senior management gathering.

5. EXTRA PREPARING AND CORRESPONDENCES ARE ADDED AS required to bond the change and make it a perpetual factor in the organization.

IT IS SIGNIFICANT THROUGH THE MAJORITY OF THIS THAT potential increments in stress levels be checked and responded to in a private manner for all staff. Done effectively, an appropriately structured and actualized change program will lessen the danger of irregular stress victory and increment efficiency by prompting a more elevated amount of pride in the organization and expanded work fulfillment at all degrees of management and staff.

WAYS TO RELIEVE STRESS IN YOUR NETWORK MARKETING Business
   We as a whole realize that stress can now and then

prevent our business and most exceedingly awful of all our health. As business visionaries a few of us have tight plans, quick moving toward due dates just as business groups we oversee, train and travel with. We additionally have families we return to after business is altogether said and done who cherish us beyond a reasonable doubt. So how might we deal with the majority of this and still have a stress free life? Well toward the day's end it's our obligation to execute a couple of practices that can enable us to carry on with a stress free life in business just as in home. When we actualize these practices on a normal it can lower or stress levels which thusly causes us become progressively profitable and productive in what we do! So here are 8 different ways you can ease stress in your system promoting business NOW!

1. DISCUSSION ABOUT WHAT STRESS YOU

When you are disappointed and feeling overpowered in your system promoting business call a companion or somebody who you can impart this to. A commonplace voice, for example, a dear companion, love one or colleague can really console you and put everything into point of view. Discussing your stress could easily compare to you think and is critical to carrying on with a healthy life.

2. TAKE ONE THING AT A TIME

As an entrepreneur or system advertiser we in some cases can take on beyond what we can bite. We attempt to deal with numerous activities, go to various preparing just as complete different errand without having a genuine calendar to pursue. When you cause a To-To do List, it makes everything somewhat more reasonable just as having a 1, 2, 3 arrangement on what you have to achieve during your day.

. . .

3. Exercise

Alright, we as a whole realize that a little exercise does a body right throughout the day. So, relating this to your stress makes it go inseparably. And whenever you are in or out of your office a touch of extending and short walk can soothe a great deal of stress. When you get the juices streaming this discharges endorphin's which get the blood siphoning and streaming and this occasionally is all you need.

4. Snicker

Chuckling improves your state of mind and diminishes stress. Consider it, have you at any point seen a stressed out individual giggling? Obviously not, that is the reason a little silliness can quiet the spirit just as the nerves. When we snicker out feelings are deceived to change over from troubled or stressed to glad and happy. In view of this chuckling is a decent solution for stress help. Viewing a satire or simply watching something senseless like this can make them chuckle in a matter of moments.

5. Unwind

Now and again we as entrepreneurs need to take a break and RELAX. This should be possible by simply kicking back without contemplating whatever manages business. A 5-15 moment breather can have a major effect in diminishing your stress. It can bring down the anxiety which thus can bring down a portion of the negative vitality that you may have within you. Additionally profound breathing while at the same time unwinding can expand the progression of oxygen which thusly can clear your head and furthermore bring down your stress levels.

. . .

6. Remain Present

One thing we should comprehend is that what is done and no compelling reason to choose not to move on. This is the reason you need to push ahead and remain present in your business. Agonizing over things you can't change just build disappointment and unneeded stress in your business. A lot to frequently we as entrepreneurs stress over past encounters that disabled person us and raise our stress levels in the present. So if you can push ahead, remain present and do what you can do now, you will discharge stress that may have been causing quite a bit of your stress.

7. Arrange

Perplexity and Clutter can cause much stress. When you are not sorted out and have no ability to know east from west life turns into a drag. Being sorted out spares you time, causes you complete undertaking just as diminishes weight, dissatisfaction. One thing I saw when I was not sorted out was that I continually surging, never on schedule and my stress level was always high. When I ended up composed I saw a 360% turn where I was consistently on schedule, not disappointed and not stressed at all since I had everything all together. So when you take a gander at being sorted out, you take a gander at having a messiness free stress less business since you made that additional move to maintain things in control.

8. Time for Self

Having opportunity to yourself is a big deal with regards to assuaging stress. A large portion of time we attempt to take on more assignment than we can deal with and some of the time this separates us. In some cases you as an entrepreneur need to disapprove of set aside a few minutes for yourself. I know as a system advertiser you need everybody to succeed and you need to be there and help out anybody you can however now and again you need to comprehend is that you need to deal with yourself too.

On the off chance that you exercise these eight different ways to calm stress on a standard you will see a more stress free you just as a prosperous business!

Straightforward Techniques to Relieve Stress - Ways to Live Happily

We all need to manage stressful circumstances - truth be told, for a considerable lot of us, stress has essentially turned into a lifestyle. Be that as it may, living with steady stress will destroy you both physically and inwardly. It is difficult to adapt to the steady flood of anxiety, weight, and dread except if you actualize stress alleviation procedures to support your body and mind rest, unwind, and restore.

Assuaging Stress is Easier than You Think

Here are some straightforward procedures to assuage stress that you can without much of a stretch utilize each day to carry on with a more stress free life:

Stay away from pointless clash. Obviously, it is beyond the realm of imagination to expect to stay away from each contradiction, yet you can utilize this strategy to help shield circumstances from ending up more awful and stressing you out significantly further.

. . .

BEFORE YOU REACT TO A TROUBLESOME INDIVIDUAL OR circumstance, take a couple of moments to consider how you can rapidly and successfully diffuse the circumstance. Regularly, the best thing to state is that you see how they're feeling and afterward ask them: "How might we make things right?" Doing this tosses the duty once more into their court and changes the discussion towards arrangement chasing.

CHOOSE WHAT YOU CAN DEAL WITH BEFORE YOU START YOUR workday. Huge numbers of us make a plunge directly into our undertakings when we land at work, without setting aside the effort to choose the amount we can deal with or what we totally need to achieve that day. The couple of minutes you go through every morning arranging your day can spare you long periods of sat around, just as sparing you a lot of stress. You don't go to an outside nation without a guide and an arrangement. The equivalent goes for your workday. Plan things out so you won't sit around idly making sense of what to do straightaway.

AGENT UNDERTAKINGS THAT OCCUPY THE MOST TIME. IT IS anything but difficult to feel like you need to deal with everything, except if you take a gander at all of the errands and activities on your plate, you will most likely find that you can designate a portion of the straightforward undertakings. Try not to be reluctant to enroll others to enable you to deal with your outstanding task at hand - this straightforward stress alleviation strategy can spare you a few hours.

GAIN FROM DISAPPOINTMENTS, HOWEVER LET GO OF THEM. Indeed, even the most gifted individuals experience disappointment every once in a while. At the point when this transpires, it is essential to discover how to improve next time, however it is similarly significant not to thrash yourself over your disappointments. Life is an adventure, not a race. Sticking to your disappointments will cause you physical and mental stress, and shield you from making the most of your triumphs.

BY UTILIZING THESE BASIC PROCEDURES TO SOOTHE STRESS, you will appreciate work and family time more, be progressively proficient and profitable, and have the option to carry on with a healthier, more joyful life.

THESE ARE ONLY A COUPLE OF PROCEDURES TO DIMINISH stress that you can use to enable you to limit the impacts of ordinary stress. Require some investment every single day to deal with all parts of your body, mind and soul. It's as basic as dodging superfluous clash, organizing what you will do every day, appointing the things you shouldn't do, and gaining from disappointments while relinquishing the things you can't change.

RELINQUISHING CONTROL

You should relinquish control to discover inner peace. This is control you have over any one in your life and power over life itself. One thing you can't do if you need peace, is give any other person control over your emotions. When you attempt to control somebody, at last they are controlling you. If you believe you have to screen's everything somebody might do, or have them be with all of you the time, you are truly confining yourself to the equivalent. You need to create trust and let go of dread.

. . .

On the off chance that you feel terrified, acknowledge it for what it is, an innocuous yet awkward feeling. No major ordeal and when you've beaten it a couple of times, it turns out to be simple. Never state "You make me feel so furious/pitiful/disappointed!" on the grounds that you are feeling those things and what another person does with their life ought not to haveeffect on you. It is tied in with creating enthusiastic knowledge and enabling individuals to carry on with their existence without being in charge of your responses.

Trust the individuals who state they cherish you and trust each collaboration you have. Try not to attempt to peruse into things, there's no point. What other individuals believe is not your issue to worry about and you will never be ensured to work it out, so simply let it go. This won't occur in a day, however continue taking a shot at yourself. Whenever you discover yourself considering what somebody says or thinks about you when you're nowhere to be found, simply try to alter your perspective to something different. And by chance, you keep doing that same thing time to time, you will in the process re-train your mind, and before you know it, you will be free from the assessments of others.

Dread for reasons unknown has been connected to such a large number of circumstances presently. Dread is really an adrenalin reaction to a circumstance we instinctually want to escape from. Anxiety, stress or stress are not fear. You might be stressed over going out in groups, you might be restless about the advancement meeting and you may feel stressed about passing without anyone else, yet you aren't apprehensive. Recognize these feelings when they emerge, let them realize they are advocated, at that point proceed with your arrangements.

REST GUARANTEED THAT THE MORE OCCASIONS YOU PROCEED, paying little mind to the sentiments, they will before long blur away. A model is a woman who hasn't dated for a long time and somebody she knows and trusts has set her up on an arranged meet up. At first she is exceptionally energized and as the time moves close, she starts to disclose to herself she is excessively apprehensive and cannot proceed with it. She winds up calling her companion for the keeps an eye on number, misleading her companions, at that point calling the man to disclose to him she has turned out to be abruptly sick and can't go. On the off chance that she just said to herself "yes this is troublesome and I AM anxious, however I can do it at any rate and anybody would be apprehensive in this circumstance, it's simply human." What is the most terrible that can occur? Perhaps she will sound or look anxious, however that is not terrible and nowhere close as inconsiderate as dropping ultimately.

DISAVOWAL RESEMBLES A SICKNESS THAT SPREADS THROUGH the minds of you and your companions. Like draws in like and you can wager your companions are more similar to you than you understand. Such a significant number of gatherings or circles bolster each other's dissents, which represses self-awareness. A model is the individuals who work in the wine business. Many are not kidding heavy drinkers and on the off chance that you ever go to a dinner party with them, you will see they all discussion about the amount they haven't been drinking, yet they drink each day. They pardon each other's gorges and rapidly attempt to change the subject if anybody raises drinking excessively. At that point there are the ones who transparently joke about being heavy drinkers together, gloating about their encounters. They are altogether hindrances to one another and they are supporting each other in their refusal.

We Can Only Change Ourselves

For what reason would anybody need to waste time with this inner peace stuff? To part of the arrangement good and bad times, feelings springing up when you don't need them as well, cooperation with others become strategic and accommodating and you will have the option to encounter an inner quiet and certainty that words cannot portray. You will never again have negligible discussions that are loaded with tattle and boasting, yet will start to discuss thoughts and occasions that are intriguing and positive. What you put out, you truly get back throughout everyday life. So if you think and feel contrarily towards others, you will ponder yourself too.

THE TIME FAMILIAR ADAGE "MIND YOUR OWN BUSINESS" IS situated in knowledge. We can just change ourselves and it isn't for us to pass judgment on the way any other person experience their lives. As we have just talked about, any judgment we make is quite identified with ourselves at any rate. Try not to burn through valuable time or vitality on what others are doing with their lives, and learn not to think about anything literally.

AT WHATEVER POINT SOMEBODY SETTLES ON A CHOICE WITH respect to how they invest their own time or vitality, it is their choice to make, so don't go putting your nose in where it isn't needed and don't contemplate you. It is extremely unlikely you can know the repercussions of your recommendation of decisions towards others, so keep your lips fixed notwithstanding when the desire appears to be overpowering to give your assessment. It isn't your place, and except if you have been overwhelmed with some amazing measure of astuteness and compulsiveness directly from the sky, you don't have the appropriate responses and shouldn't act as you do.

SELF-ACKNOWLEDGMENT IS SIGNIFICANT AND YOU NEED TO recall not to be difficult for yourself. We are largely here on this planet learning and becoming regular. When you initially start to open your eyes and become increasingly self-mindful, you may begin to feel a freshly discovered feeling of disgrace, humiliation, resistance or insufficiencies. This is something worth being thankful for. The initial step to recuperating is to see the issues and issues you have. At that point you are in a spot where you can work from. Be happy to grasp your shortcomings and understand these are your issues to survive so you can encounter self-improvement. Experiencing life thinking you are immaculate isn't the best approach to pick up anything and it is through tough occasions, preliminaries and difficulties that you truly develop. Be set up to dedicate yourself completely to circumstances where you will commit errors, as you will likely get familiar with the most about yourself.

SELF-ACCEPTANCE

Consider setting aside the effort to compose a rundown of the things you dread most throughout everyday life. At that point genuinely consider ways you can move in the direction of going up against and beating those feelings of dread. You should add to your rundown as you become increasingly self-mindful, on the grounds that you will have more acknowledge concerning what your identity is and what you can take a shot at surviving. A few models may be if you are terrified of specific feelings in others, you cannot acknowledge compliments, you can't give compliments, and you are awkward with friendship, investing energy alone, ascending stepping stools, felines, hounds, and so forth, and so on.

WHEN COMPOSING THE RUNDOWN, TAKE A GANDER AT YOUR responses to circumstances and recollect dread isn't simply felt as dread and is frequently camouflaged as outrage. An ideal model is the mother who can't discover her kid for a couple of minutes. A fear comes over her and when she finds the person in question, she responds in an irate manner and hollers at that person for leaving. It's an over response and is anything but a genuine articulation of her feelings. The dread stays smothered and unacknowledged, so may be intensified next time a comparable circumstance emerges.

IN ALL YOU DO, YOU MUST BE EAGER TO BE STRAIGHTFORWARD with yourself as well as other people. On the off chance that you can't be straightforward, you will be not able discover synchronicity in your life. Envision you were concentrating a night course at school and you were truly battling with a task you had due very soon. You were too humiliated to even think about asking anybody in your group for assistance and were, rather, attempting to attempt to understand your examination. Just by some coincidence, you happen to chance upon your teacher at the grocery store and he asks you how you are getting along on your task. Since you feel frail and embarrassed to concede you need assistance, you state "fine thanks", change the subject and surge off. If you were straightforward and said you were truly battling with this one, he would most likely say dropped by and see me and we will go over it and check whether you can figure out how to comprehend it better. It is so imperative to consistently be in your fact and not be embarrassed about what your identity is or what others may think, as it can keep you down as you continued looking for inner peace.

A TIME FOR REFLECTION

Give yourself an opportunity to think about your self-improvement. On the off chance that you never get tranquil occasions to think and let what is on your mind risen to the top, your mind will turn out to be extremely occupied with contemplations that are yet to be managed. Consider it a normal support for your mind and soul, regardless of whether it's an hour daily or a day seven days, you need to give yourself that blessing to keep up your health.

YOU HAVE TO PERCEIVE AND ALWAYS REMIND YOURSELF THAT material things don't bring genuine bliss. Any satisfaction you do get is fleeting and shallow. You should have the option to find a sense of contentment with yourself with just what you have to endure and see everything else as a little something extra, without getting to be connected to it. The familiar axiom "you can't take it with you" is a great idea to recall.

THE REASON YOU CAN'T SIMPLY CHOOSE TO HAVE INNER PEACE is that, regardless of how hard you attempt, if you haven't taken the necessary steps to clear your stuff and resolve your issues, they will cause issues down the road for you. You might have the option to go a day or a week or even two or three months feeling just as you find a sense of contentment, yet your stifled feelings and musings will eject and presumably when you least need them to.

Choose today to relinquish your personality, have a decent useful take a gander at yourself and your life and decide to a beginning gaining from others. It is the voyage not the goal that is the most charming and important. When you start to chip away at the way to inner peace, you will discover you need to keep advancing and changing for a mind-blowing remainder.

CHAPTER FIVE

How to Manage Thoughts to Control Anxiety

Anxiety can cause physical indications like a quick heartbeat and sweat-soaked hands. It can make you limit your exercises and can make it difficult to make an amazing most.

Healthy thinking can enable you to forestall or control uneasiness.

- Negative thoughts can expand your stress or dread.
- CBT, is a sort of treatment that can assist you supplant negative considerations with precise, empowering ones.
- Changing your thinking will take some time. You have to rehearse sound reasoning each day. Sooner or later, solid reasoning will work out easily for you.
- Healthy thinking may not be sufficient to help a few people who have stress and uneasiness. Call your primary mindfulness physician or advisor if you think you need more help.

How might you utilize healthy thinking to adapt to anxiety?

- **Notice and stop your thoughts**

The initial step is to notice and stop your negative thoughts or "self-talk." Self-talk is the thing that you ponder yourself and your encounters. It resembles a running editorial in your mind. Your self-talk might be objective and accommodating. Or on the other hand it might be negative and not supportive.

- **Get some information about your considerations**

The following stage is to ask yourself whether your musings are useful or unhelpful. See what you're stating to yourself. Does the proof help your negative idea? A portion of your self-talk might be valid. Or on the other hand it might be halfway evident however misrepresented.

Perhaps the most ideal approaches to check whether you are stressing an excessive amount of is to take a gander at the chances. What are the chances, or possibilities, that the awful thing you are stressed over will occur? If you have a vocation audit that has one little analysis among numerous compliments, what are the chances that you truly are in risk of losing your employment? The chances are likely low.

There are a few sorts of unreasonable contemplations. Here are a couple of types to search for:

•**Focusing on the negative:** This is some of the time called sifting. You channel out the great and spotlight just on the terrible. Model: "I get so apprehensive talking openly. I simply realize that individuals are considering how terrible I am at speaking." Reality: Probably nobody is more centered around your exhibition than you. It might search for some proof that beneficial things occurred after one of your introductions. Did individuals hail a short time later? Did anybody reveal to you that you worked admirably?

•**Should:** People once in a while have set thoughts regarding how they "should" act. On the off chance that you hear yourself saying that you or other individuals "should," "should," or "need to" accomplish something, at that point you may set yourself up to feel terrible. Model: "I must be in charge constantly or I can't adapt to things." Reality: There's nothing amiss with needing to have some authority over the things that you can control. In any case, you may cause yourself nervousness by agonizing over things that you can't control.

•**Overgeneralizing:** This is taking one model and saying it's valid for everything. Search for words, for example, "never" and "consistently." Example: "I'll never feel typical. I stress over everything constantly." Reality: You may stress over numerous things. Be that as it may, everything? Is it conceivable you are misrepresenting? In spite of the fact that you may stress over numerous things, you likewise may find that you feel solid and quiet about different things.

•**All-or-nothing thinking:** This is additionally called dark or-white reasoning. Model: "On the off chance that I don't find an ideal line of work audit, at that point I'll lose my employment." Reality: Most execution surveys incorporate some useful analysis—something you can chip away at to improve. On the off chance that you get five positive remarks and one useful proposal, that is a decent survey. It doesn't imply that you're in risk of losing your employment.

•**Catastrophic thinking:** This is accepting that the most exceedingly terrible will occur. This kind of unreasonable reasoning regularly incorporates "imagine a scenario where" questions. Model: "I've been having cerebral pains of late. I'm so stressed. Consider the possibility that it's a brain tumor?" Reality: If you have loads of migraines, you should see a specialist. However, the chances are that it's something progressively normal and far less genuine. You may need glasses. You could have a sinus contamination. Possibly you're getting strain cerebral pains from pressure.

- **Choose your thoughts**

The following stage is to choose an accommodating idea to supplant the unhelpful one.

Keeping a diary of your contemplations is probably the most ideal approaches to work on halting, asking, and picking your musings. It makes you mindful of your self-talk. Record any negative or unhelpful considerations you had during the day. On the off chance that you figure you probably won't recall them toward the finish of your day, keep a scratch pad with you so you can record any considerations as they occur. At that point record accommodating messages to address the negative musings.

If you do this consistently, precise, supportive contemplations will before long work out easily for you.

However, there might be a trace of validity in a portion of your negative musings. You may have a few things you need to deal with. On the off chance that you didn't execute just as you might want on something, record that. You can take a shot at an arrangement to address or improve that zone.

- **Ways to Calm Your Anxious Mind**

Anxious thoughts can overpower you, settling on it hard to settle on choices and make a move to manage whatever issue troubles you. Anxiety can likewise prompt overthinking, which makes you increasingly restless, which prompts more overthinking, etc. How might you escape this endless loop? Subduing on edge considerations won't work; they will simply spring up once more, now and then with greater power. However, there are progressively viable procedures you can acquire from mindfulness-based pressure decrease and CBT.

Coming up next are 9 methods to enable you to get unstuck and push ahead:

1. Attempt Cognitive Distancing

Attempt to consider your to be contemplations as conjectures, not as certainties. Your mind is attempting to secure you by foreseeing what could occur—however in light of the fact that something could happen doesn't mean it will. See target proof: How likely is it that the negative result will really occur? Is there anything great that may occur? What's more, which do you believe is well on the way to occur, in light of past involvement and other data you have about the circumstance?

2. Attempt Cognitive De-Fusion

Quit being intertwined with your contemplations. Think about your musings as moving information going through your brain, as opposed to the target truth about a circumstance. Our brains are extremely touchy to risk and threat since this kept our predecessors alive in nature. A portion of your contemplations may simply be programmed molded responses created by a mind that is situated to endurance. Pick whether to accept these contemplations, as opposed to simply tolerating them.

3. Practice Mindfulness

Work on watching your musings, as opposed to responding consequently to them. Think about your musings as mists gliding by. Which attract you and which make you need to flee? Is there a way you can unwind yourself and simply watch your musings, as opposed to responding?

4. Concentrate on Direct Experience

Your mind makes up anecdotes about what your identity is, and about your wellbeing and adorableness. Not these accounts are exact. Now and again our minds are one-sided by negative past encounters. What is your involvement right now? Is this something that is really occurring or something that may occur? Notice that they are not something very similar, despite the fact that your brain may regard them as the equivalent.

5. **Label Things**

Label the sort of thought you are having, as opposed to focusing on its substance. Watch your musings and when you see a judgment (e.g., how fortunate or unfortunate the circumstance is), feel free to mark it as Judging. On the off chance that you see a stress (e.g., that you will fizzle or experience a misfortune) mark it as Worrying. If you are scrutinizing yourself, name it as Criticizing. This gets you away from the exacting substance of your contemplations and gives you more consciousness of your psychological procedures. Would you like to invest your energy judging and stressing? Are there less judgmental or stressed approaches to see the circumstance?

6. **Stay in the Present**

Is your mind disgorging the past? Because something negative occurred in the past doesn't mean it needs to happen today. Inquire as to whether the conditions, or your insight and adapting capacities, have changed since the last time. As a grown-up, you have progressively decision about whom to connect with and greater capacity to recognize, acquire, or leave an awful circumstance than when you were a youngster or adolescent.

7. **Widen Your View**

It is safe to say that you are concentrating too barely on the compromising parts of a circumstance, as opposed to seeing the entire picture? Uneasiness makes our brains agreement and spotlight on the quick danger without thinking about the more extensive setting. Is this circumstance truly as significant as your uneasiness says it seems to be? Will despite everything you mindfulness about this issue in 5 or 10 years? On the off chance that not, at that point simplicity up on the stress.

8. **Get Up and Get Going**

Stressing over an issue without making an answer won't enable you to take mindfulness of the issue. It might in certainty make you less inclined to act by sustaining your uneasiness. At the point when your mind is stuck in a circle, you can interfere with it by getting up and moving around or doing an alternate assignment or movement. At the point when you sit down, you ought to have an alternate point of view.

9. DECIDE WHETHER A THOUGHT IS HELPFUL

Because an idea is genuine doesn't imply that it is useful to concentrate on—at any rate not constantly. On the off chance that lone 1 out of 10 individuals will land the position you look for, and you continue considering those chances, you may move toward becoming demotivated and not by any means try applying. This is a case of an idea that is valid however not supportive. Concentrate on what is useful and released the rest!

How to Manage your Activities to Reduce Anxiety

I HAD AN "AH HA" MINUTE A YEAR AGO THAT HAS COMPLETELY changed me. Or possibly the discernment I have of my life.

Like such a significant number of individuals, I was occupied, occupied, occupied. I was shuffling heaps of balls noticeable all around without a moment's delay... two small kids, a business, a house to oversee, charitable effort to do, also tennis, my Bunco gathering and Book Club, without any end in sight. I would begin the day running and regularly fall in bed after 12 PM with just 50% of my plan for the day confirmed. "One week from now things will settle down" I'd let myself know, just to find that one week from now was similarly as occupied. I was continually anticipating when things would back off - yet that time never showed up.

Sound natural? I wager it does in light of the fact that I infrequently meet individuals who aren't pushed and overpowered attempting to complete everything.

We live in a harried, depleted society. Furthermore, I had fallen prey to the conviction that occupied is great - it implies I am beneficial, and NOT lethargic. I've even ended up boasting (camouflaged as whimpering) about the fact that I was so occupied to other people. Once in a while, I'd get into a benevolent challenge with somebody to see who was the "busiest." Now, that is crazy!

We don't get decorations for destroying ourselves - we simply get depleted!

At that point, it hit me one day. My life is occupied - however more significantly it is FULL. I am accomplishing such a significant number of things that I need to do in light of the fact that they make me glad and they fit my vision. Rather than saying, "I have a truly bustling week "- I began supplanting "occupied" with "full" - and all of a sudden, my viewpoint changed. I have an "entire week." I have a "full life". Brimming with exercises that help my family, give me reason, empower me, and are charming.

That may appear to be an extremely little and basic activity. Yet, changing that single word likewise changed my point of view - and that is POWERFUL! I started to settle on a cognizant decision to perceive the magnificence in my life. I perceived that I was so blessed to have such a significant number of chances, connections, and encounters. I remembered I would prefer not to lounge around staring at the TV and eating bon bons (in any event, not more often than not). I need a full life - brimming with joy, love and fulfillment.

I understood that everything in my life is a decision. I pick the individuals and the exercises that fill my days. Subsequently, it us up to me to settle on savvy decisions and be certain I am picking things that are satisfying and not only things to make me occupied.

At that point, I began looking nearer and when something came up that didn't feel better - that didn't feel "full" to me - I chose I expected to release that thing. Gradually, I began saying "no" to the things that weren't satisfying. Presently, when I start to feel worried by my calendar, I recognize that I am so fortunate to accomplish such a significant number of things that I cherish

Anxiety can influence your body, mind and conduct. Here are some useful tips* for overseeing anxiety by tending to these three territories.

I propose you choose a couple to begin with that appear to be most pertinent to you.

- **Healthy body**

Physical manifestations of anxiety can incorporate muscle strain, dashing heart, dazedness, perspiring, and brevity of breath. These can happen out of the blue and be very upsetting. They can be anticipated or decreased by customary self-mindfulness and unwinding.

1: **Nurture Yourself**

- Eat standard well-adjusted dinners (for example three nutritious suppers daily).
- Avoid or lessen liquor, nicotine, and caffeine admission.
- Exercise routinely, especially with a cardiovascular or unwinding part.

- Perform customary self-mindfulness -, for example, loosening up exercises and normal arranged breaks.
- Have a decent rest schedule.

2: **Breathe**

Breathing admirably can back off or interfere with the uneasiness reaction, and give a feeling of quiet, establishing, or unwinding.

- Practice cognizant profound relaxing for 1 moment at once, at whatever point you are hanging tight for something (for example holding up in line, for a test to begin, when halted at a traffic light).
- Try protracting your exhalation or outward breath - take in for 4 seconds and inhale out for 5 or 6 seconds. Practice this cycle a couple of minutes every day, or at whatever point you consider it.

3: **Be Mindful**

Monitoring our body and surroundings in a non-judgmental way can lessen sentiments of nervousness and bring a condition of quiet.

- Close your eyes and watch your breathing: see your body, how the admission of air feels and what sensations you watch.
- Shift your attention to what you can hear, smell, and contact, monitoring nature outside your body.
- Shift mindfulness to and fro from your body to your surroundings a few times.

4: **Use Cues to Relax**

At the point when you know that your body is tense or

you feel that you can't relinquish stress or stress, utilize this as a prompt to rehearse increasingly standard unwinding.

- Try fixing and discharging diverse muscle gatherings, to work on loosening up the ones that are generally tense.
- Imagine when you inhale out that any strain in your body is streaming outward, and as you take in, envision it is being supplanted by warmth, vitality, and harmony.
- Think of a picture or scene that is unwinding to you, and picture this when feeling tense or under pressure.
- Schedule normal unwinding and charming exercises -, for example, rub, steaming showers, work out, or being in nature.

- **Healthy mind**

Anxiety can be joined by mental action that is upsetting, diverting and inefficient. This incorporates stress and distraction with fears or envisioned negative results. The more you stress, the more it is probably going to happen.

5: **Be Realistic**

Regularly when individuals are restless, they think about the most noticeably awful conceivable result to their circumstance, regardless of whether this is probably not going to happen. This builds nervousness and its belongings.

- Notice if you are pondering your indications or circumstance.
- Remind yourself that emotions are not actualities - in light of the fact that you fear a specific result,

doesn't make it bound to happen or make your stresses work out.
- Employ rationale - challenge yourself to think about a result or end that is not so much cataclysmic, but rather more liable to happen as a general rule. You may need to request that others help in the beginning. Record your reaction as a future update.
- Think of times in the past when your stresses have refuted.

6: INTERRUPT ANXIOUS THINKING

Now and again it's difficult to utilize coherent reasoning, particularly when uneasiness is high. Brief disturbance of on edge musings can enable you to get to your rationale and pick what you would like to concentrate on.

- Identify if perpetual and capricious stress for sure 'if?' believing is an issue for you.
- Try some extraordinary (and senseless) approaches to interfere with this negative procedure, for example,
- Sing your stresses to a senseless tune, or talk them in an entertaining animation voice.
- Pick a charming idea to concentrate on or envision, for example, something you anticipate or are pleased with doing.
- Listen to music or a book recording.
- Intentionally return your consideration regarding the assignment you are performing, advising yourself that stress is unhelpful.

7: **Contain Your Worry**

If your stress is difficult to control, diverts you from your day by day undertakings, and expends your reasoning, attempt a few different ways to restrict the stress and permit yourself a break.

- Identify if your stress is reasonable (includes an angle inside your control) or unsolvable (outside of your control).
- Use critical thinking to concentrate on reasonable stresses. Unmistakably distinguish the issue, conceptualize potential arrangements, use experts and con leans to choose the best solution(s), and make an activity arrangement to address the issue.
- For unsolvable stresses, use unwinding and different methods to lessen your negative response to the circumstance.
- Worry well and just once - utilize a stress diary or journal to list your stresses once per day (up to 20mins). When and if those stresses re-happen during the day, advise yourself that you have just stressed over that today.
- Imagine a vacant compartment to store your stresses - envision yourself setting your stresses into this, naming them as you go, at that point rationally put on the top. Welcome a quiet idea or re-center onto the assignment you are dealing with.

8: Coach Yourself to Approach Situations

Some nervousness is ordinary throughout everyday life, except maintaining a strategic distance from things in regular day to day existence that we dread just makes uneasiness more grounded. On the off chance that we can approach esteemed yet anxiety inciting circumstances, they become simpler after some time and with training.

- Assess your shirking - know about spots and circumstances you maintain a strategic distance from because of uneasiness however which you might want to approach.
- Rate your dread of these on a 1 to 10 scale (with 1 being low degrees of anxiety and 10 being the most noteworthy conceivable uneasiness). The objective of instructing is to diminish this dread.
- Assess your self-talk - What unhelpful things would you say you are educating yourself concerning the circumstance which increment anxiety?
- List your objectives - How is shirking meddling with these? Record what you might want to do if anxiety was not in the manner.
- Begin to rehearse in little portions enduring some anxiety without attempting to escape it promptly (you may require some assistance with this if your levels are high).
- Practice instructing yourself in increasingly helpful articulations to counter negative self-talk for example 'I may feel on edge yet I am as yet ready to do this.' Think of events when you have adapted well or when the dreaded result has not happened. Record them to help remind you.

- **Healthy behavior**

In conquering anxiety, it is generally insufficient to change our considerations alone. Improving the way, we oversee pressure and approach nervousness inciting circumstances can frequently be the most significant advance.

9: **Reduce Over-Activity**

A few people accomplish more when on edge. While high movement can lessen anxiety for the time being, as you may accomplish a few objectives, it can compound nervousness in the long haul as you feel over-worked and overpowered.

- Check if over-movement is an issue for you:
- Do you want to be continually occupied?
- Do you think that it's difficult to back off or unwind and get increasingly on edge when you have spontaneous spare time?
- Make a rundown of thoughts for back-up exercises during surprising available time, ideally a scope of unwinding or pleasant exercises (for example go to the craftsmanship exhibition, read a book) with a scope of terms. During an unforeseen extra time, pick one from your rundown.
- Do not do assignments that are not your duty. Some of the time, enable others to add to assignments or help you, regardless of whether you accept they won't do it the manner in which you would.
- Practice doing little undertakings incompletely (for example purposefully miss a spot when clearing the floor, or forget about a full-stop in an article). This will feel awkward, yet will enable you to loosen up additional by diminishing your emphasis on pointless subtleties.
- Balance your time - Use a journal, calendar, or pie-graph to follow how you are investing energy in various territories. Ensure the classes that are essential to you are incorporated for example rest, eating, work out, social/connections, work, study, etc.
- Laugh and have a fabulous time - a progressive thought, however work on giggling from your paunch. Have close by certain things that make you

snicker (for example interesting pictures, messages) for use on distressing days.

10: **Make a Plan and Practice**

To feel certain and skilled utilizing the procedures you have picked, make an arrangement to rehearse these normally so they can turn out to be new, sound propensities.

- Learn about uneasiness. It will lessen if you can unlearn the dread through great adapting encounters.
- Become well-polished at fast quieting strategies, for example, profound relaxing for use when on edge.
- Set important objectives for your life and recognize the aptitudes you have to accomplish these. Discover where/how you can get familiar with these abilities, and expand on them through training. Get help with this on the off chance that it appears to be overwhelming. Start with one little advance (the least terrifying) to approach your objective, and practice this until you feel prepared to attempt the following level.
- Remember that nothing is immaculate - mishaps will happen and this is ordinary. Consider what you could realize and do any other way later on. Alter your arrangement if necessary.

CHAPTER SIX

Ways to Find Instant Calm and Overcome Anxiety

While it's entirely expected to get apprehensive about a significant occasion or life change, anxiety disorder is common among nearly 40 million Americans, which is more than the incidental stress or dread. Anxiety disorder can extend from a GAD, which is serious stressing that you can't control, to panic disorder - abrupt scenes of dread, alongside heart palpitations, trembling, shaking, or perspiring.

FOR THOSE WITH AN ANXIETY DISORDER, IT'S IMPERATIVE TO investigate techniques that can help oversee or lessen anxiety in the long haul, similar to talk treatment or medicine. Yet, everybody can profit by different approaches to diminish pressure and anxiety with way of life changes, for example, setting aside effort for yourself, eating regimen, and eating a well-adjusted restricting liquor and caffeine. Additionally, there are steps you can take the minute when uneasiness begins to grab hold. Attempt these 10 master upheld proposals to loosen up your mind and help you recapture control of your contemplations.

1. REMAIN IN YOUR TIME ZONE.

Anxiety is a future-situated perspective. So as opposed to stressing over what will occur, "reel yourself back to the present,". Ask yourself: What's presently going on? Am I safe? Do I need to do something right now? If not, make a "plan" to check in with yourself later in the day to come back to your anxieties so those far away circumstances don't lose you track, she says.

2. RELABEL WHAT'S HAPPENING.

Panic attack can frequently make you have an inclination that you're passing on or having a coronary episode. Remind yourself: "I'm having a fit of anxiety, however it's innocuous, it's brief, and there's nothing I have to do," Mickey says. Besides, remember it truly is something contrary to an indication of approaching passing - your body is initiating its battle or-flight reaction, the framework that is going to keep you alive, she says.

3. FACT-CHECK YOUR THOUGHTS.

Individuals with anxiety frequently focus on most pessimistic scenario situations, Mickey says. To battle these stresses, consider how sensible they are. How about we accept that you're anxious about a significant presentation at work. As opposed to might suspect, "I'm going to bomb," for instance, say, "I'm anxious, yet I'm readied. A couple of things will go well, and some may not," she proposes. Getting into a case of reevaluating your feelings of trepidation causes train your brain to think of an objective method to manage your anxious contemplations.

4. TAKE IN AND OUT.

Deep breathing causes you quiet down. While you may have found out about explicit breathing activities, you don't have to stress over checking out a specific number of breaths, Mickey says. Rather simply center around equitably taking in and breathing out. This will help deferred down and re-center brain, she says.

5. FOLLOW THE 3-3-3 RULE.

Look at you and name three things you see. By then, name three sounds you hear. Finally, move three bits of your body - your fingers, lower leg, and arm. The moment you feel your brain going 100 miles for consistently, this mental trick can help center your mind, returning you to the present moment, Mickey says.

6. JUST DO SOMETHING.

Go for a stroll, Stand up, discard a bit of rubbish from your work area - any activity that intrudes on your line of reasoning encourages you recapture a feeling of control, Mickey recommends.

7. STAND UPRIGHT.

"At the point when we are restless, we guarantee our chest region - where our heart and lungs are found - by slumping over," Mickey says. For a speedy physical solution for this typical reaction, pull your shoulders back, stand or sit with your feet isolated, and open your chest. This causes your body begin to detect that it's back in charge, she says.

8. Avoid sugar.

It may lure to follow something sweet when you're centered, yet that chocolate bar can achieve more harm damage than anything else, as research demonstrates that eating an excessive amount of sugar can exacerbate restless emotions. Instead of wandering into the treat bowl, drink a glass of water or eat protein, Mickey says, which will give a moderate imperativeness your body can use to recover.

9. Ask for a second opinion.

Text or call a companion or relative and go through your stresses with them, Mickey opines. "Saying them so anyone can help you to recognize the truth about them plainly." It can in like manner make your emotions out of fear on paper.

10. Watch an interesting movie.

This last technique may be the most straightforward one yet: Cue up catches of your preferred entertainer or clever TV appear. Snickering is a decent solution for an anxious mind, Mickey says. Research demonstrates that giggling has loads of advantages for our emotional wellness and prosperity; one investigation found that amusingness could help lower nervousness as much as (or significantly beyond what) exercise can.

Coping With Symptoms of Anxiety Excessive Worrying

At the point when you end up stressing, ask yourself the accompanying inquiries:

Is Your Worry Reasonable?

Is the thing you dread extremely liable to occur? How might you be certain? Is there another conceivable clarification or result? Is it true that you are attempting to foresee things in the removed future that you can't in any way, form or shape anything about? If it does occur, what amount of will it truly matter? How might another person see this stress?

WHAT IS THE EFFECT OF THINKING THE MANNER YOU ALWAYS DO?

If your stress has some premise, yet there is nothing you can do about it at the present time, at that point check whether you can acknowledge the stress and let it go. This can appear to be hard for master worriers, yet attempt to state "There's nothing I can do to change this at this moment, pondering it will just make me increasingly furious. I'll acknowledge the stress and get occupied with something different for the time being".

IS THERE A REAL PROBLEM TO BE SOLVED?

On the off chance that there is a reasonable issue, at that point you may need to concentrate on discovering answers for it. Great critical thinking can be thought of as supportive or versatile stress.

ATTEMPT THE SIX-STEP STRUCTURED PROBLEM-SOLVING Technique

- Write down precisely what you accept the primary issue to be.
- Write down every single imaginable arrangement,

even awful ones.
- Think about every arrangement in down to earth terms.
- Choose the most down to earth arrangement.
- Plan how you will complete that arrangement.
- Do it.

Did that help you take mindfulness of the issue? If not, have you taken in a superior method for characterizing it? Assuming this is the case, record the new issue and do the six stages once more. This is in the same class as drug for some individuals.

CHAPTER SEVEN

Mindfulness Meditation

Regardless of whether you're pondering family life, work, school, what you're going to make for supper, what you said finally night's gathering, or the entirety of the above mentioned, it's anything but difficult to get trapped in an example of twirling considerations. Now and then we ruminate on past occasions—even to the degree that it prompts uneasiness—or we center around the could-be circumstances of things to come.

Mindfulness reflection is a psychological preparing practice that can be useful in these circumstances. It brings you and your contemplations into the present, concentrating on feelings, considerations, and vibes that you're encountering "in the now." While it very well may be at first hard to calm your musings, with time and practice you can encounter the advantages of mindfulness reflection, including less pressure and nervousness, and even a decrease in indications of conditions like IBS.

Mindfulness systems can change, however as a rule, mindfulness reflection includes a breathing practice, mental symbolism, familiarity with body and mind, and muscle and body unwinding.

Beginning a Mindfulness Meditation Practice

One of the first institutionalized projects for mindfulness contemplation is the Mindfulness-Based Stress Reduction (MBSR) program, an understudy of Buddhist priest and researcher Thich Nhat Hanh. His eight-week program guides understudies to focus on the present, decline reactivity and excitement, and accomplish a condition of quiet. Other progressively disentangled, mainstream mindfulness reflection mediations have been progressively consolidated into therapeutic settings to treat stress,1 pain,2 and depression3 among different conditions.

Learning mindfulness reflection is clear enough to rehearse individually, yet an instructor or program can assist you with beginning, especially in case you're rehearsing contemplation for explicit wellbeing reasons. While a few people ruminate for longer sessions, even a couple of moments consistently can have any kind of effect. Here's an essential strategy to assist you with beginning:

1.Find a peaceful and agreeable spot. Sit in a seat or on the floor with your head, neck, and back straight however not firm. It's additionally useful to wear open to apparel so you're no occupied.

2.Try to set aside all memories and the future and spotlight on the present.

3.Become mindful of your breath, adjusting to the vibe of air moving all through your body as you relax. Feel your tummy rise and fall and the air enter your noses and leave your mouth. Focus on the manner in which every breath changes and is unique.

4.Watch each thought go back and forth, regardless of whether it be a stress, dread, tension, or expectation. At the point when considerations come up in your mind, don't disregard or smother them. Essentially note them, keep quiet, and utilize your breathing as a grapple.

5.If you wind up becoming overly enthusiastic in your considerations, see where your mind headed out to, without judgment, and simply come back to your relaxing. Keep in mind not to be difficult for yourself if this occurs.

6.As the opportunity arrives to a nearby, sit for a moment or two, turning out to be mindful of where you are. Get up slowly.

Consolidating Mindfulness Into Your Daily Life

There's no law that says you should sit on a pad in a peaceful space to rehearse mindfulness, says Kate Hanley, creator of "A Year of Daily Calm." Mindfulness reflection is one strategy, however regular exercises and undertakings give a lot of chances to rehearse.

Here are Hanley's tips on developing mindfulness in your every day schedule.

Washing the Dishes

Have you at any point seen how nobody is attempting to stand out enough to be noticed while you're doing the dishes? The blend of alone time and dull physical movement causes tidying to up after supper an extraordinary time to attempt a little mindfulness. Enjoy the sentiment of the warm water on your hands, the vibe of the air pockets, the hints of the dish thumping on the base of the sink.

Zen educator Thich Nhat Hanh calls this activity "washing the dishes to wash the dishes"— not to get them over with so you can go stare at the TV. At the point when you give yourself over to the experience, you get the psychological refreshment and a spotless kitchen.

Brushing Your Teeth

You can't go a day without brushing your teeth, making this undertaking the ideal every day chance to rehearse mindfulness. Feel your feet on the floor, the brush in your grasp, and your arm going all over.

Driving

It's anything but difficult to daydream while you're driving, pondering what to have for supper or what you neglected to do at work that day. Utilize your forces of mindfulness to keep your consideration tied down to within your vehicle. Mood killer the radio—or put on something relieving, similar to old style music—envision your spine developing tall, locate the midpoint between loosening up your hands and grasping the wheel too firmly, and at whatever point you see your mind meandering, take your consideration back to where you and your vehicle are in space.

Working out

Sitting in front of the TV while running on the treadmill may cause your exercise to go all the more rapidly, yet it won't do a lot to calm your brain. Flex both your physical and mental muscles by killing all screens and concentrating on your breathing and where your feet are in space as you move.

Getting ready for Bedtime

Rather than racing through your night schedule and doing combating with your children over sleep time, attempt to appreciate the experience. Get down to a similar level as your children, look in their eyes, listen more than you talk, and enjoy any cuddles. At the point when you unwind, they will as well.

Mindfulness is the fundamental human capacity to be completely present, mindful of where we are and what we're doing, and not excessively receptive or overpowered by what's happening around us.

It's not all in your mind—you can rehearse mindfulness by plunking down for a conventional reflection practice, or by being increasingly purposeful and mindful of the things you do every day.

And when you need to get familiar with mindfulness and

how to rehearse mindfulness reflection, visit our Getting Started page.

The most effective method to Practice Mindfulness in a hurry

About each undertaking we perform in a day—be it brushing our teeth, having lunch, conversing with companions or working out—should be possible all the more mindfully.

At the point when we are aware of our activities, we give more consideration to what we are doing. It's something contrary to making a cursory effort—rather, you are fixed on your faculties, seeing your musings and feelings.

By building mindfulness into your day by day life, you can rehearse mindfulness in any event, when you're too occupied to even think about meditating.

Figuring out How to Meditate

At the beginning, it sets a measure of time no doubt about it "practice" for. Else, you may fixate on choosing when to stop. In case you're simply starting, it can pick a brief timeframe, for example, five or ten minutes. Inevitably, you can develop to twice as long, at that point perhaps as long as 45 minutes or 60 minutes. Utilize a kitchen clock or the clock on your telephone. Numerous individuals do a session in the first part of the day and at night, or either. And when you feel your life is occupied and you have brief period, showing improvement over doing none. At the point when you get a little reality, you can do more.

Locate a decent spot in your home, in a perfect world where there isn't a lot of messiness and you can locate some tranquil. Leave the lights on or sit in common light. You can even sit outside and when you like, however pick a spot with little interruption.

This stance practice can be utilized as the starting phase of a time of contemplation practice or just as something to accomplish for a moment, possibly to balance out yourself and discover a snapshot of unwinding before returning into the conflict. If you have wounds or other physical challenges, you can change this training to suit your circumstance.

Step by step instructions to Sit for Mindfulness Meditation

1.Take your seat. Anything that you're perched on—a seat, a reflection pad, a recreation center seat—discover a recognize that gives you a steady, strong seat, not roosting or waiting.

2.Notice what your legs are doing. And when on a pad on the floor, fold your legs easily before you. (And when you as of now do some sort of situated yoga pose, proceed.) If on a seat, it's great if the bottoms of your feet are contacting the floor.

3.Straighten—yet don't solidify—your chest area. The spine has regular ebb and flow. Give it a chance to be there. Your head and shoulders can serenely lay over your vertebrae.

4.Situate your upper arms parallel to your chest area. At that point let your hands drop onto the highest points of your legs. With your upper arms at your sides, your hands will arrive in the correct spot. Excessively far forward will make you hunch. Excessively far back will make you firm. You're tuning the strings of your body—not very tight and not very free.

5.Drop your jawline a little and let your look fall tenderly descending. You may allow your to eyelids lower. If you feel the need, you may bring down them totally, yet it's not important to close your eyes while reflecting. You can basically let what shows up before your eyes be there without concentrating on it.

6.Be there for a few seconds. Unwind. Carry your consideration regarding your breath or the sensations in your body.

7.Feel your breath—or some state "pursue" it—as it goes out and as it goes in. (A few variants of this training put more accentuation on the outbreath, and for the inbreath you just leave a roomy delay.) Either way, cause you to notice the physical vibe of breathing: the air traveling through your nose or mouth, the rising and falling of your midsection, or your chest. Pick your point of convergence, and with every breath, you can rationally note "taking in" and "breathing out."

8.Inevitably, your consideration will leave the breath and meander to different places. Try not to stress. There's no compelling reason to square or kill thinking. At the point when you get around to seeing your mind meandering—in almost no time, a moment, five minutes—just delicately return your thoughtfulness regarding the breath.

9.Practice delaying before making any physical changes, for example, moving your body or scratching a tingle. With aim, move at a minute you pick, permitting space between what you experience and what you decide to do.

10.You may discover your mind meandering continually —that is typical, as well. Rather than grappling with or drawing in with those musings to such an extent, work on seeing without expecting to respond. Simply sit and focus. As hard all things considered to keep up, that is everything that matters. Return again and again without judgment or desire.

11.When you're prepared, delicately lift your look (if your eyes are shut, open them). Notice any sounds in the earth. Notice how your body feels at the present time. Notice your considerations and feelings. Briefly stopping, choose how you'd like to proceed with your day.

That is it. That is the training. It's regularly been said that it's straightforward, however it's not really simple. The work is to simply continue doing it. Results will collect.

OTHER MEDITATION TECHNIQUES

There are different other contemplation methods. For instance, a day by day contemplation practice among Buddhist priests centers straightforwardly around the development of sympathy. This includes imagining negative occasions and recasting them in a positive light by changing them through empathy. There are likewise moving contemplation strategies, for example, yoga, qigong, and strolling reflection.

Advantages OF MEDITATION

And when unwinding isn't the objective of contemplation, it is regularly an outcome. During the 1970s, Herbert Benson, MD, an analyst at Harvard University Medical School, authored the expression "unwinding reaction" subsequent to leading exploration on individuals who rehearsed supernatural reflection. The unwinding reaction, in Benson's words, is "an inverse, automatic reaction that causes a decrease in the action of the thoughtful sensory system."

The objective of reflection is to center and comprehend your mind—in the end arriving at a more elevated level of mindfulness and internal quiet. Reflection is an antiquated practice, however researchers are as yet finding the entirety of its advantages. Ordinary reflection can assist you with controlling your feelings, improve your focus, decline pressure, and even become progressively associated with people around you. [1] With training, you'll have the option to accomplish a feeling of serenity and harmony regardless of what's happening around you. There are various approaches to ponder, so and when one practice doesn't appear to work for you, consider attempting an alternate kind that works better for you before you surrender.

Types of meditation

Meditation is an umbrella term for the numerous approaches to a casual condition of being. There are numerous sorts of contemplation and unwinding methods that have reflection parts. All offer a similar objective of accomplishing internal harmony.

Approaches to ruminate can include:

Guided contemplation. Now and then called guided

symbolism or representation, with this technique for reflection you structure mental pictures of spots or circumstances you find unwinding.

You attempt to use however many faculties as would be prudent, for example, smells, sights, sounds and surfaces. You might be driven through this procedure by a guide or instructor.

Mantra reflection. In this kind of reflection, you quietly rehash a quieting word, thought or expression to avoid diverting musings.

Mindfulness contemplation. This sort of contemplation depends on being mindfulness, or having an expanded mindfulness and acknowledgment of living right now.

In mindfulness reflection, you expand your cognizant mindfulness. You center around what you experience during contemplation, for example, the progression of your breath. You can watch your musings and feelings, however let them go without judgment.

Qi gong. This training by and large joins reflection, unwinding, physical development and breathing activities to re-establish and look after parity. Qi gong (CHEE-gung) is a piece of customary Chinese drug.

Judo. This is a type of delicate Chinese hand to hand fighting. In judo (TIE-CHEE), you play out a self-guided arrangement of stances or developments in a moderate, elegant way while rehearsing profound relaxing.

Supernatural Meditation®. Supernatural Meditation is a straightforward, regular strategy. In Transcendental Meditation, you quietly rehash a by and by doled out mantra, for example, a word, sound or expression, with a particular goal in mind.

This type of reflection may enable your body to subside into a condition of significant rest and unwinding and your mind to accomplish a condition of internal harmony, without expecting to utilize focus or exertion.

Yoga. You play out a progression of stances and controlled breathing activities to advance a progressively adaptable body and a quiet personality. As you travel through represents that require equalization and fixation, you're urged to concentrate less on your bustling day and more on the occasion.

Attempting Basic Meditation Practices

Pursue your relaxing. The most fundamental and widespread of all reflection strategies, breathing contemplation , is an incredible spot to begin your training. [15] Pick a spot over your navel and spotlight on that spot with your mind. Become mindful of the rising and falling of your mid-region as you take in and out. Try not to try to change your breathing examples. Simply inhale regularly.

Attempt to concentrate on your breathing and just your relaxing. Try not to consider your breathing or pass any kind of judgment of it (e.g., "That breath was shorter than the last one."). Simply endeavor to know your breath and know about it.

Concentrate on mental pictures to direct your relaxing. Envision a coin sitting on the spot over your navel and rising and falling with every breath. Or then again picture a float gliding in the sea that is weaving all over with the grow and break in your relaxing. On the other hand, envision a lotus bloom sitting in your tummy and spreading out its petals with each admission of breath.

Try not to stress if your mind begins to meander. You are a learner, and contemplation takes practice. Simply endeavor to refocus your brain on your breathing and attempt to consider nothing else.

Rehash a mantra to enable you to center.

Mantra contemplation is another regular type of reflection that includes rehashing a mantra (a sound, word, or expression) again and again until you quiet the mind and enter a profound, thoughtful state. The mantra can be anything you pick, insofar as it's anything but difficult to recollect.

Some great mantras to begin with incorporate words like "one," "harmony," "quiet," "serene," and "quietness."

If you need to utilize increasingly customary mantras, you can utilize "Om," which symbolizes inescapable awareness. Or then again you can utilize the expression "Sat, Chit, Ananda," which signifies "Presence, Consciousness, Bliss ."

Quietly rehash the mantra again and again to yourself as you ponder, enabling the word or expression to murmur through your mind. Try not to stress if your mind strays. Simply refocus your consideration and refocus on the reiteration of the word.

As you enter a more profound degree of mindfulness and cognizance, it might get pointless to keep rehashing the mantra.

Have a go at focusing on a straightforward visual book to assuage pressure. Along these lines to utilizing a mantra, you can utilize a straightforward visual book to center your mind and enable you to arrive at a degree of more profound cognizance. This is a type of open-eye contemplation, which numerous meditators find supportive.

The visual item can be anything you wish. The fire of a lit light can be especially lovely. Other potential books to consider incorporate precious stones, blooms, or pictures of celestial creatures, for example, the Buddha.

Spot the item at eye level, so you don't have to strain your head and neck to see it. Look at it until your fringe vision begins to diminish and the item expends your vision.

When you are centered totally around the item, you should feel a feeling of significant tranquility.

Practice representation if you like to concentrate internal. Representation is another famous contemplation system. One basic sort of representation includes making a serene spot in your brain and investigating it until you arrive at a condition of complete quiet. The spot can be anyplace you like; be that as it may, it ought not be totally genuine. You need to envision a remarkable spot that is customized for you.

The spot you picture could be a warm, sandy sea shore, a blossom filled glade, a tranquil woods, or a happy with living room with a thundering fire. Whatever place you pick, enable it to turn into your asylum.

When you have rationally entered your haven, enable yourself to investigate it. Try not to work to "make" your environment. Maybe they are as of now there. Simply unwind and enable the subtleties to go to the front line of your mind.

Take in the sights, sounds, and aromas of your environment. Feel the crisp breeze against your face or the warmth of the flares warming your body. Appreciate the space for whatever length of time that you wish, enabling it to normally grow and turn out to be progressively unmistakable. At the point when you are prepared to leave, take a couple of full breaths, at that point open your eyes.

You can return to this equivalent spot whenever you practice representation, or you can basically make another space.

Do a body sweep to discover and discharge strain. Doing a body filter includes concentrating on every individual body part thus and deliberately loosening up it. To start, sit or rests in an agreeable position. Close your eyes and start to concentrate on your breathing, at that point bit by bit move your consideration starting with one part of your body then onto the next. Notice the sensations you feel as you go.

You may think that its supportive to begin at the base and stir your way up. For instance, focus on whatever sensations you can feel in your toes. Try to loosen up any contracted muscles and discharge any strain or snugness in your toes. At the point when your toes are completely loose, move upwards to your feet and rehash the unwinding procedure.

Proceed with your body, moving from your feet to the highest point of your head. Invest as a lot of energy as you like concentrating on each piece of your body.

When you have finished the unwinding of every individual body part, center around your body in general and appreciate the impression of serenity and detachment you have accomplished. Concentrate on your relaxing for a few minutes before leaving your contemplation practice.

With normal practice, this procedure can make you increasingly mindful of the different sensations in your body and assist you with managing them fittingly.

Attempt heart chakra contemplation to take advantage of sentiments of adoration and empathy. The heart chakra is one of 7 chakras, or vitality focuses, situated inside the body. The heart chakra is situated in the focal point of the chest and is related with affection, sympathy, harmony, and acknowledgment. Heart chakra reflection includes connecting with these sentiments and sending them out into the world. To start, get into an agreeable position and spotlight on the vibes of your relaxing.

As you become progressively loose, envision a green light transmitting from your heart. Envision the light filling you with an impression of unadulterated, brilliant love.

Picture the adoration and light emanating all through your whole body. From that point, enable it to emanate outward from your body and enter the universe around you.

Take a couple of seconds to just sit and feel the positive vitality inside and around you. At the point when you're set, step by step enable yourself to get mindful of your body and your breath once more. Tenderly squirm your fingers, toes, and appendages, at that point open your eyes.

Have a go at strolling contemplation to unwind and practice simultaneously. Strolling contemplation is a substitute type of reflection that includes watching the development of the feet and getting mindful of your body's association with the earth. If you plan on performing since quite a while ago, situated reflection sessions, have a go at separating them with some strolling contemplation.

Empower yourself to transform into your own special calm passerby and simply watch the breath. As you seek after each take in and inhale out, thoughts will end up being all the more moderate. Permit the to contemplations come and release them, basically watching them and not getting the chance to be associated with them. Your middle is the breath, reliably return to the cadenced take in and inhale out. By then empower yourself to transform into the breath. With this solidifying comes release and without a veritable transient affirmation you are submerged in stillness, in the calm and you have discovered the puzzle gap. This is the spot of being, of value and of your real self. Here you are at one with everything on the side; paying little mind to whether that be God, universe, Tao, divine mindfulness or whatever your term for it is, you are it, it is you and it and you are everything.

Would I have the option to show myself; do I need an educator?

Contemplation is a journey of self disclosure inciting self predominance that you can start as of now - today. There is nothing you need to find that you don't have straightforwardly starting at now inside you. Simply sit and empower yourself to be. It is troublesome, setting up the upset monkey mind that races beginning with one thought then onto the following regardless, with preparing, it transforms into a welcomed opportunity to contribute vitality with yourself.

A reflection teacher can help and guide you through the demonstration of contemplation and setting off to a social event reflection session will enable you to bestow the experience to other individuals, which can bolster your own one of a kind preparing. In any case, I would urge you to start practicing yourself as I have depicted around there. There is nothing a contemplation teacher can unveil to you that you don't have any acquaintance with, you just need to sit and be with yourself to discover it.

Consolidating Meditation into Your Everyday Life

Attempt to ruminate simultaneously consistently. Planning your reflection practice for a similar time every day will assist it with turning out to be a piece of your ordinary daily practice. If you contemplate day by day, you'll experience its advantages all the more significantly.

Early morning is a decent time to contemplate since your mind has not yet become overcome with the anxieties and stresses of the day.

It's anything but a smart thought to think straightforwardly subsequent to eating. In case you're processing a dinner, you may feel awkward and less ready to think.

Take a guided contemplation class to sharpen your procedures. And when you need extra direction, consider taking a reflection class with an accomplished educator. You can discover a scope of various class types via looking through on the web.

Neighborhood rec centers, spas, schools, and devoted reflection focuses offer classes in numerous areas.

You can likewise locate a wide scope of guided reflections and instructional recordings on YouTube.

For an increasingly vivid encounter, investigate going to an otherworldly retreat where you will go through a few days or weeks in escalated reflection. Vipassana Meditation offers free multi day withdraws at focuses all through the world.

Peruse profound books to study reflection. In spite of the fact that not for everybody, a few people find that perusing profound books and consecrated compositions encourages them get contemplation and moves them to take a stab at internal harmony and otherworldly understanding.

Some great books to begin with incorporate A Profound Mind: Cultivating Wisdom in Everyday Life by the Dalai Lama, The Nature of Personal Reality by Jane Roberts, "A New Earth" by Eckhart Tolle, and One-Minute Mindfulness by Donald Altman.

And when you wish, you can choose components of knowledge that impact you from any otherworldly or consecrated messages and think about them during your next reflection session.

Practice mindfulness in your regular day to day existence. Contemplation doesn't need to be constrained to your training sessions. You can likewise rehearse mindfulness during your time to-day life. Essentially take a shot at monitoring what's going on both inside and around you at some random minute for the duration of the day.

For instance, in snapshots of stress, attempt to take a couple of moments to concentrate exclusively on your breathing and void your mind of any negative contemplations or feelings.

You can likewise rehearse mindfulness when you eat by getting mindful of the nourishment and every one of the sensations you experience as you eat.

Regardless of what activities you perform in your day by day life—whether it's sitting at a PC or clearing the floor—attempt to turn out to be increasingly mindful of your body's developments and how you feel right now. This concentration and mindfulness is living mindfully.

Have a go at establishing activities to assist you with being progressively present. Establishing is a procedure to assist you with rehearsing mindfulness in regular day to day existence. You should simply concentrate straightforwardly on something in your environment or a particular sensation in your body.

For instance, you may concentrate on the blue shade of a pen or envelope on a table close to you or look at all the more intently the sentiment of your feet on the floor or your hands laying on the arms of your seat. Take a stab at doing this if you have an inclination that you are occupied or you discover your mind is meandering, or and when you are feeling focused.

You can likewise give centering a shot various sensations without a moment's delay. For instance, get a keyring and focus on the sounds the keys clear, the manner in which they feel in your grasp, and even their metallic smell.

Keep up a solid way of life notwithstanding pondering. While reflection can improve your general wellbeing and prosperity, it works best and when you join it with other sound way of life rehearses. Attempt to eat strongly, practice , and get enough rest .

Abstain from observing an excess of TV, drinking liquor, or smoking before reflection. These exercises are undesirable, and they can numb the brain—keeping you from accomplishing the degree of focus fundamental for fruitful reflection.

View contemplation as a voyage instead of an objective. Reflection isn't an objective that you can finish, such as attempting to get an advancement at work. Survey contemplation similarly as a device to accomplish a specific objective (regardless of whether you will probably be edified) would resemble saying the objective of a walk around a lovely day is to walk a mile. Concentrate rather on the procedure and experience of contemplation itself, and don't bring the wants and connections that occupy you in everyday life into your reflection practice.

When starting, you shouldn't be excessively worried about the nature of the contemplation itself. For whatever length of time that you feel more settled, more joyful, and more settled toward the finish of your training, your reflection was effective.

Reflection doesn't need to be detailed. Take in. Breath out. Give your stresses a chance to liquefy away. Simply unwind.

If you think that its hard to ponder for the period of time you have picked, attempt a shorter time for some time. Nearly anybody can reflect for 1-2 minutes without encountering meddling contemplations. At that point, as the sea of the mind quiets, you can progressively stretch your contemplation session until you have accomplished the ideal time span.

It is difficult to think when you're initially starting a reflection practice. You'll become accustomed to it once you begin to ponder normally. Take as much time as is needed and show restraint toward yourself.

Do what works best for you. One individual's optimal contemplation system may not be the best one for you. Analysis with various practices to locate the ones you like best.

What you do with a quiet personality is up to you. A few people find that it is a decent time to present a goal or an ideal result to the subliminal personality. Others want to "rest" in the uncommon quietness that reflection offers. For strict individuals, contemplation is frequently used to interface with their god(s) and get dreams.

Advantage of reflection

1. You get familiar at using sound judgment.

In case you're worried regularly, you've most likely had those minutes throughout your life where you settled on awful choices thus. Regardless of whether it's subtleties you missed for a significant task or a major botch you made that contrarily influenced other individuals, you comprehend what it resembles when you're not at your best.

What's being debilitated in minutes like this is an aptitude called official capacity.

Basically, official capacity is the piece of your brain that encourages you get results for objectives you are attempting to accomplish. It's what encourages you accomplish things like deal with your time, focus, plan, sort out and recollect subtleties.

Studies have demonstrated convincing proof that it helps individuals who have debilitated official working abilities from conditions, for example, Attention-deficiency/hyperactivity issue (ADHD).

A study run by Dr. Lidia Zylowska indicated 78% of grown-up members with ADHD encountered a decrease of generally speaking ADHD side effects when they routinely utilized reflection rehearses.

2. You become a specialist at taking mindfulness of pressure.

Snapshots of stress triggers your amygdala, otherwise called your "reptile brain". It's the base piece of your mind which is related with dread and feeling and its essential capacity is to enable you to endure.

Elevated levels of pressure can cause you to go into reptile brain mode where it is overwhelmed by the amygdala. It tends to be depicted when one "flips his top" and is constrained by overpowering feeling, for example, dread or outrage. Consider it times you've been in a warmed contention or ghastly smindfulnessd of something that may hurt you.

At the point when you are in this mode, other significant pieces of your mind like the pre-frontal cortex, which is the piece of your brain that is fit for more elevated level speculation, for example, basic leadership, mindfulness, sympathy and profound quality, are killed

Since the amygdala isn't as extraordinary at intelligent suspecting for the less clear circumstances of every day life, contemplation can help decline your feelings of anxiety by first getting you out of your reptile brain and back to being right now, which at that point enables you to react to worry in a greatly improved manner.

For instance, you may be in reptile mind mode considering how to make due by getting more cash, however through contemplation, you interface with what's generally significant in spite of all the pressure. You understand before it's past the point of no return that you've been disregarding the more significant things like associating with your children and keeping up closeness with your mate.

X-ray checks have indicated that following an eight-week course of mindfulness practice, the amygdala seems to recoil. What's more, as the amygdala contracts, the pre-frontal cortex gets thicker.

Fundamentally, science has demonstrated that contemplation can assist you with getting better at taking mindfulness of your worry by enacting the piece of your mind that settles on better choices.

3. You normally recall valuable data.

Envision a period where you disclosed to yourself a rundown of things you needed to purchase at the market without physically recording it. When you get to the store, you've overlooked what a portion of those things were.

This is the point at which your working memory limit has missed the mark. You utilize your working memory when you have to put a clingy note in your mind with the goal that you can utilize it sooner rather than later. The issue is in some cases those clingy notes tumble off when you need it.

If your working memory is the data that goes on these psychological clingy notes, at that point your working memory limit is to what extent you can have these clingy notes remain on before it tumbles off. The more drawn out time you need to hold data, the additional time you have for thinking and cognizance to happen.

Contemplation has been appeared to improve your working memory limit.

One study had around 200 adolescents doled out to either a mindfulness reflection practice, yoga, or were hold up recorded as a control gathering. Results indicated that the adolescents taking an interest in the contemplation bunch had essentially preferred working memory limit over those taking an interest in different gatherings.

4. You become an astonishing smooth talker.

If you've at any point had when you were conversing with somebody and you experienced difficulty finding the correct words to express what you were attempting to state, you've had a minute where your verbal familiarity wasn't busy's ideal.

Verbal familiarity as characterized by verbal expertise master, Min Liu, is the "capacity to locate the correct words at the ideal time or in the correct circumstance."

At the point when sixty-three University of North Carolina, Charlotte understudies with no reflection experience volunteered for a test that concentrated the impacts of contemplation on their verbal familiarity, results indicated that there was a noteworthy improvement in verbal familiarity with the individuals who occupied with mindfulness reflection versus the individuals who didn't. What's more, to add to these noteworthy outcomes, the gathering who contemplated just did it for 20 minutes every day more than multi day time frame.

5. You create laser-like core interest.

With all the data readily available in this advanced age, it's anything but difficult to get occupied. We are presented to a normal of 10,000 promoting commercials daily and it's difficult to observe what the significant things we should concentrate on are. The fake A.D.D. culture we've made has caused us to have essentially shorter capacities to focus because of data over-burden .

Taking as meager as 20 minutes every day for five days to take part in think has improved one's consideration, which shows the intensity of essentially making an unpretentious move and spending a modest portion of your day just being available.

6. You superpower your mind.

All the mark folds you see on the external surface on the mind that resemble breezy streets have been shaped to help increment the speed of synapse correspondence. The arrangement of these folds is known as gyrification. Since your brain doesn't have any space inside your skull to get greater, it experiences gyrification to expand the limit of your mind work.

Long haul meditators have been appeared to have a bigger measure of gyrifcation contrasted with the individuals who don't rehearse contemplation. All the more strangely, an immediate connection was found between the measure of gyrification and the quantity of reflection years, which is confirmation of the capacity of our mind to keep developing even as grown-ups.

This implies the more you reflect, the quicker and increasingly proficient your mind becomes at preparing data, which can be particularly helpful in minutes where you have to think quick. (Looking at intuition quick, a Digital Brain like this will really profit your mental ability a great deal!)

7. You are better at critical thinking.

At the point when your brain is taking mindfulness of a difficult issue, it requires the expertise to concentrate consideration on what's generally significant among a lot of data.

A basic case of your mind at work participating in such compromise is the point at which you're at a noisy gathering conversing with a companion. If your mind didn't distinguish and resolve all the clashing incitement around you by helping you overlook all the clamor around you and spotlight on your companion, you'd most likely have a tactile over-burden.

A similar chief applies when you run into bigger compromise difficulties. You should have the option to figure out what's generally significant and concentrate on it.

Numerous studies have demonstrated that members in bunches who participated in contemplation rehearses had performed higher on assessments that tried compromise abilities contrasted with bunches that didn't.

This demonstrates why the individuals who contemplate by and large have a lower anxiety. Their brains are increasingly capable at compromise.

8. Your imagination begins to prosper.

The Harvard Business Review has directed investigations that have indicated that 10-12 minutes of mindfulness contemplation rehearses were sufficient to support inventiveness. Most of members who were a piece of the reflection arm of the investigation announced that it helped them "clear their brains, center more around the main job, and think of unique arrangements."

Mindfulness reflection gets thoughts streaming legitimately to your neocortex, which is the place the entirety of your innovative reasoning happens. It's nothing unexpected why the absolute most driving organizations have presented contemplation in the work environment accordingly:

"The Walt Disney Company was an early adopter of reflection in the work environment, as they saw an emotional increment in inventiveness after representatives thought about imaginative arrangements. General Mills is another organization which reports improved development because of sitting in stillness and has reflection rooms accessible to their staff. Google has an in house mindfulness program called 'Search inside Yourself' and has constructed a maze for mindfulness strolling reflections."

9. You execute your nervousness and experience more harmony.

About 6.8 million Americans experience the ill effects of General Anxiety Disorder (GAD) and regardless of whether you're not one of them, odds are you at any rate stress over something on most days.

When stressing turns into a typical piece of your day by day life, it can negatively affect you and you wind up losing rest, being tense and have a hustling mind that won't sit still.

Contemplation has been for quite some time built up as a cure for tension. Analysts at Wake Forest Baptist enlisted fifteen sound volunteers with ordinary degrees of regular nervousness to try out this hypothesis.

The members had no past reflection experience. In the wake of taking part in four 20-minute mindfulness reflection classes, it was accounted for that nervousness was discernibly diminished in each session that they ruminated.

The brain imaging examines taken of these individual uncovered that reflection was giving uneasiness alleviation by initiating the foremost cingulate cortex which is one piece of the mind that assists with the control of stress. Sweeps additionally uncovered declines in the dark matter of the amygdala which is the piece of the brain that assumes a significant job in nervousness and stress.

10. Your brain remains youthful for eternity.

The vast majority of the neurons in your mind are contained inside a part known as dark issue. It's inside the dark issue where fundamental things, for example, memory, feelings, discourse, basic leadership, and discretion happen.

After you arrive at 30-years of age, your brain starts to gradually contract. In any case, proof shows that the individuals who keep their mind fit as a fiddle by participating in standard contemplation practices can counteract the contracting out and out.

One study from UCLA demonstrated that in long haul meditators, age-related dark issue misfortune was less articulated contrasted with the individuals who didn't contemplate.

Mind sweeps of the members who had been thinking for a normal of 20 years even demonstrated more dim issue volume all through their brain than anticipated.

11. You become incredible at adjusting to changes.

Psychological adaptability is the crucial capacity that has been portrayed as the capacity to adjust practices in light of changes happened in the earth.

Suppose you began to live in another nation, your degree of intellectual adaptability will decide how quick you can acclimate to every one of the progressions to your condition, for example, having the controlling wheel on the contrary side of the vehicle, learning the neighborhood language and making sense of the subtleties of the new culture.

Meditators performed essentially superior to non-meditators as inspected in an examination which brought members through activities that tried subjective adaptability. The examination demonstrated that mindfulness is firmly connected to enhancements to psychological adaptability.

So in case you're consistently experiencing difficulty changing in accordance with another circumstance, perhaps a little contemplation will tackle your concern.

12. You start to win your fight with the blues.

An exploration survey distributed in the Journal of the American Medical Association (JAMA) of Internal Medicine in January 2014 demonstrated contemplation was about as compelling as an energizer.

Another concentrate on mindfulness contemplation distributed by analysts from the University of Exeter saw it as superior to medications or guiding for sadness. They found that following four months of thinking, about 75% of patients felt alright to quit taking antidepressants.

Regardless of whether you aren't experiencing clinical discouragement, contemplation will inspire your state of mind in case you're feeling down.

13. You develop more grounded and experience less agony.

Mindfulness contemplation has been appeared in clinical preliminaries to decrease interminable torment by 57 percent and that prepared meditators can lessen it by more than 90 percent. Mind check contemplates show that reflection can physically modify the structure of the brain so it never again feels torment at a similar degree of power.

Emergency clinic torment centers currently recommend mindfulness reflection to help patients experiencing a wide range of sicknesses, for example, malignant growth, joint inflammation and coronary illness.

Much the same as numerous different investigations looking into reflection benefits, you can see the aftereffects of contemplation inside a brief timeframe outline regardless of whether you've never done it.

Wake Forest University led an examination that took 15 sound members and performed brain filters while initiating torment. An ensured teacher took them through mindfulness reflection throughout the following four days and by the fifth day, there was around a 40 percent decrease in torment power evaluations while they were thinking contrasted with when they weren't.

14. Your capacity of poise goes up another level.

If you've at any point wound up surrendering to the enticements of eating that tub of frozen yogurt when you're on diet or illuminating that cigarette when you're attempting to stop, contemplation may be the accurate thing you have to give you that additional push of discretion.

Indeed, contemplation can even assist individuals with

recuperating from different kinds of addictions. Reflection actuates the front cingulate and prefrontal cortex which are simply the pieces of your brain identified with poise.

One study demonstrated that smokers who were allocated to complete 5 hours of contemplation spread more than about fourteen days indicated a 60% decrease in smoking contrasted with the smokers who didn't ponder.

15. You increase a general feeling of satisfaction up another level.

And when you've at any point encountered the pleasurable experience of the "sprinters high," at that point you recognize what it feels like to have an arrival of endorphins in your brain. While endorphins are synapses that your body utilizes as a characteristic painkiller, it's likewise liable for the general feeling of joy you at times feel.

At the point when an examination looked at 11 first class sprinters and 12 exceptionally prepared meditators, results indicated that the two gatherings had discernibly raised degrees of endorphins subsequent to running and reflection. All the more curiously, the pleasurable impacts of endorphin discharge were estimated in these gatherings and the contemplation bunch scored higher.

What's surprisingly better is that when you contemplate, you really set aside a few minutes and space to think about your motivation and what persuades you. What's more, know what? At the point when you do discover your motivation of living, you become much more joyful!

AFTERWORD

We have established the legitimate nature of mind isn't exactly what you understand or conceive in your own mind or your own being at that moment. When something goes and you perceive its own motion, what goes? It's the matter that goes, not your mind. If it's possible to stabilize your numerous minds by discovering the way they take you enjoy a puppy on a leash together with all the happenings of earth, then you are going to start to listen on your one true head. Only through diligent attempts in accepting the slides you think about yourself, largely that you understand exactly what you are and you understand the essence of mind, are you going to discover there is just 1 fact, only then can you start the job. Until then, it isn't the flag that waves in the end, nor the end which moves , but it's the mind that moves.

To say there's just 1 reality would be to state the many realities which folks claim to get, are only illusions. Whatever you understand to be a fact is just a subjective illusionary perspective of a few of the numerous moving minds which take you apart in your one non-moving mind. Fighting for what you believe , or safeguarding your perspectives and opinions would be like hanging on the anchor of this ship lost in the center of the sea.

Unless you're prepared to offer up the notion that you know whatever, then you won't have the ability to go through the character of your mind since we mentioned, that's unthinkable. Should you hold to some beliefs, or into the concept which you have any notion of reality or truth, you then prohibit the thoughts from becoming empty and , that's the sole means to go through the character of the one true head. You can't locate truth in case you maintain a lie to be fact.

Funny enough, if you let go of your false senses of fact, such as the one which you understand your thoughts, or the understanding that you feel you think that you don't know your thoughts (both are equivalent trixters), you'll have all understanding, since you've reached the one true head that's everywhere at all times.

This route can take several decades, and since you advance step by step, you might acquire certain skills, but you must be warned to not believe you've attained the amount of complete understanding of the true mind, so there will probably always be a trixter waiting at the shadows. When you buy it done, you may know, and you won't be in a position to describe or specify it.

Exercise being the stone in the storm, never moving. You'll find this difficult it seems to be hopeless, and you're likely perfect. It probably will be hopeless for you, or just any human being to attain ideal enlightenment. Nonetheless, it's extremely possible to enhance the condition of the being. So don't become discouraged from performing some other practices since you're able to observe the immense task ahead, just make it your own destination and attempt to get as near as possible. One step nearer remains a step nearer. Better for a little stone transferred than a foliage ruined.

Made in the USA
Monee, IL
08 August 2020